DIFFERENTIATING
the High School
Classroom

DIFFERENTIATING
the High School
Classroom

Solution Strategies for 18 Common Obstacles

KATHIE F. NUNLEY

CORWIN PRESS
A SAGE Publications Company
Thousand Oaks, California

For information:

Corwin Press
A Sage Publications Company
2455 Teller Road
Thousand Oaks, California 91320
www.corwinpress.com

Sage Publications Ltd.
1 Oliver's Yard
55 City Road
London EC1Y 1SP
United Kingdom

Sage Publications India Pvt. Ltd.
B-42, Panchsheel Enclave
Post Box 4109
New Delhi 110 017 India

Printed in the United States of America.

Library of Congress Cataloging-in-Publication Data

Nunley, Kathie F.
Differentiating the high school classroom: Solution strategies for 18 common obstacles / Kathie F. Nunley.
       p. cm.
Includes bibliographical references and index.
ISBN 1-4129-1715-8 (cloth) — ISBN 1-4129-1716-6 (pbk.)
   1. Individualized instruction. 2. Mixed ability grouping in education.
3. High school teaching. I. Title.
LB1031.N85 2006
371.39′4—dc22   2005019386

This book is printed on acid-free paper.

05   06   07   08   09   10   9   8   7   6   5   4   3   2   1

Acquisitions Editor:	Faye Zucker
Editorial Assistant:	Gem Rabanera
Production Editor:	Diane S. Foster
Copy Editor:	Bonnie Freeman
Typesetter:	C&M Digitals (P) Ltd.
Proofreader:	Joyce Li
Cover Designer:	Michael Dubowe
Graphic Designer:	Scott Van Atta
Cartoonist:	Diane Eudy

Contents

Acknowledgments

I must take this rare opportunity to thank Faye Zucker at Corwin Press for making this book happen. She has amazing perseverance and weathered much to get this book from concept to print.

A deep-felt thank-you also to Diane and Micheal, who are two of the most special people in my life and who have done so much to support me in a myriad of ways throughout my adult life. While I frequently tell Diane how much I love and appreciate her and her support, I am lax in saying that often enough to Micheal. So Micheal, thank you for your time, creativity, and perspective.

Finally, the two most influential men in my life need a special thank-you here. My husband, Kevin has been my support and guide and without him none of this would ever have happened. Last, a quick thank-you goes to my Dad. He gave me my value system, taught me right from wrong and the importance of each, and that it is okay to take time to just have fun. Thank you also for introducing an impressionable little 11-year-old girl to a man called Don Quixote whose words continue to be a great inspiration:

> *This is my quest, to follow that star . . .*
>
> *No matter how hopeless, no matter how far.*
>
> *To fight for what's right, without question or pause.*
>
> *To be willing to march into hell for a heavenly cause.*
>
> *For I know, if I'll only be true to this glorious quest,*
>
> *that my heart will lie peaceful and calm, when I'm laid to my rest.*
>
> *And the world will be better for this.*

Corwin Press thanks the following individuals for their contributions to this work:

William Fitzhugh, Teacher, Reisterstown Elementary School, Reisterstown, MD

Steve Hutton, Instructor, Kentucky Department of Education, Villa Hills, KY

Toby Karten, Educational Consultant, College of New Jersey, Marlboro, NJ

Millie Murray-Ward, Assistant Provost for Assessment, California Lutheran University, Thousand Oaks, CA

J. David Smith, Professor of Education and Psychology, University of Virginia's College of Wise, Pound, VA

Jacqueline Thousand, Professor, Cal State San Marcos, San Marcos, CA

About the Author

Kathie F. Nunley, EdD, delights teachers from around the world with her practical solutions to the challenges of today's diverse classrooms. With more than 15 years of high school classroom teaching experience in both urban and suburban schools, she is the developer of the Layered Curriculum method of instruction. Dr. Nunley is a noted speaker at state, national, and international conferences and has authored several books and articles on brain biology and teaching in the mixed-ability classroom. A mother of four, she continues her brain research, writing, and educational consulting from her 1800s farmhouse in New England.

*This book is dedicated to the wildlife of the
Allegheny Mountains—the dragonflies, pileated woodpeckers,
turtles, wild turkey, screaming eagles, the cacophony of frog voices,
salamanders, black bear, raccoon, and deer. They all provided inspiration
during the writing of this book by allowing me the experience of a different kind
of diversity. In the wilderness or in the classroom, every creature brings unique gifts
from above. Beauty is to be found in the blending of those gifts. Celebrate the symphony.*

Introduction:
I Just Can't Do
That in MY School/
Classroom/Situation

Teachers and the teaching profession have problems. No one disputes that. Put a group of teachers in a room, and our favorite topic of discussion is undeniable: problems! Let's just get them out of the way right now.

We don't have enough books.

We don't have enough chairs.

We don't have enough power outlets.

The technology doesn't work.

We have no funds for materials.

Our class sizes are too big.

Our absentee rates are too high.

Our students don't come to class prepared.

We cannot get parent involvement.

We get too much parent involvement.

We don't get parental support.

The legislature mandates new programs but forgets to fund them.

Our per pupil expenditure is too low.

The fire drill went off at the wrong time.

There are too many assemblies.

The athletes were pulled from seventh period—again!

I can't get an administrator in my room.

I can't get an administrator out of my room.

There are more native languages than students in my room.

The paperwork is overwhelming.

I have five separate preps this year.

They've locked the supply room.

The copy machine is out of order.

They just told me I'm coaching girls' soccer.

I can't be sick; we have no subs.

Whew. I'll bet you could fill another 10 pages with problems I haven't even mentioned. And they are all very legitimate and valid problems.

Let me state a strong philosophy of mine right up front. I subscribe to the 80-20 rule for problems. When there is a problem, let's spend 20 percent of our time, effort, and energy describing and discussing the problem and 80 percent of our time, effort, and energy discussing and looking for solutions.

So let's start by accepting that yes, there are problems in education and the teaching profession. This book will touch on some. Accept problems as part of the professional calling we all heard. Now let's really put our energy into some solutions. Absolutely anyone can talk about problems, but it takes real skill and creativity to work out solutions.

TEACHERS ARE CREATIVE PEOPLE

The tougher the problem, the more creative we must be. When teachers share with me the various difficult situations they are in, I respond, "Rejoice—you've been given a wonderful opportunity to show your ingenuity and creative genius."

Struggles build character and intelligence. I once consulted for a school at a state correctional institution. The teachers there could have textbooks, ruled 8½ × 11 inch notebook paper, and golf pencils in their room. That's it. Yes, golf pencils, those stubby pencils with no eraser. (Erasers apparently could be chewed into some kind of gummy thing and put in the locks.) They did get chalk and a chalkboard, but the chalk was kept under lock and key.

Could you teach geometry, biology, U.S. history, art, or whatever discipline you excel in, in a creative manner at this school? Could you use lots of hands-on activities and differentiate to this very high-risk population with very low literacy skills?

Your response is probably similar to what mine was: "Wow, we better get creative!"

Opportunity knocks in mysterious ways. Take advantage. Or as my father always said, "You have to play the cards you're dealt."

I've tried in my adult life to stay focused on the positive, focused on the solutions. The tougher it gets, the more I call on my creative juices.

LAUGH AND THE WORLD LAUGHS WITH YOU

One of the easiest ways to start your creative juices flowing is by finding the humor in any situation. Even when enmeshed in some extremely trying circumstances, try to find a reason to laugh, at yourself and the situation. You know the old adage, "If you don't laugh, you'll cry." Well, it may apply to your world some days.

People are often amazed that I can make fun of my adult life and laugh at my situation. But I do—on a very regular basis. I laugh at myself and about my children and my classroom. At first glance many events in my adult life may seem quite tragic. I look at all these events as golden opportunities. And I'm the first to admit that I've had more than my share of golden opportunities. For, you see, I am a regular education teacher but a special-education parent with a penchant for brain research and biology.

I must include in this introduction a bit of personal history so that you can better see my bias and perspective on this topic of inclusion and differentiated instruction. Thus far, you know me as a writer. But in my spare time I am also the mother of four children. I have one of everything. Literally no matter how you view it, I have a little of everything. I have one in college, one in high school, one in middle school, and one in elementary school. I have one African American, one Native American, and two Irish Americans. I have three boys and one girl. I have one with autism, one with traumatic brain injury, and one with dyslexia. I have one Boy Scout, one Girl Scout, one engineer, and one runner. I have one math genius, one sleepwalker, one actor, and one plain ol' crazy kid. I've been surrounded by research projects in regular and special education.

I'll also mention here that, just for fun, in my backyard I also have 28 chickens. Actually 27 hens and one rooster, named Ed. My daughter named the rooster "King Edward" as a youngster, then "Mean Ol' Ed" when Ed got older. (If you've ever raised chickens, you know how mean the roosters get when they grow up.) Ed had a stroke last summer and lost the use of one of his legs, so now he's a one-legged rooster we call "Special Ed."

I promise I'm not making any of this up. So you see, you can't scare me—I've seen it all.

My research projects began more than 20 years ago. Unable to have children, we adopted a son. After six years of waiting, our son arrived as a beautiful, 14-day-old baby, who turned out to have autism. The

trials and tribulations of raising my son could fill a book (and one day will, I hope). I'll save the details of life with Keegan for another book, but I will mention here that I learned a few things from raising a son with autism. Did you know they don't generalize well? They take things literally. So when your son wakes up with a scratchy throat one morning, do not say to him, "Keegan, I think you're a little hoarse this morning," because if you do, you'll get a response like "you mean I'm not a little boy anymore!?"

After a few more years and miracles, we were able to adopt a daughter. Our beautiful new baby girl appeared to be finishing her first year as "completely normal"—much to our delight. Her first birthday was celebrated in a neighboring city with extended family. On the icy drive home on the interstate, a drunk driver hit us head-on. The bulk of the car came in on our daughter, and our beautiful little girl lost areas of her frontal lobes.

Before I had children, my brain research focused on serial killers. My master's project compared premeditated murderers with affective murderers. At the time, THAT seemed interesting to me. Needless to say, the focus of my brain research changed with motherhood.

Now rearing two special education children, my research on the brain took two new directions. While at the time I did not fully appreciate the value of the situation, what a wonderful opportunity I have had to look at and work with autism and other pervasive development disorders as well as traumatic brain injury and brain plasticity.

My grandmother would tell me, "Kathie, the good Lord doesn't give us more than we can handle. But I'm praying for you. I pray to Him every day to leave you alone!"

After 15 years of marriage and several years of raising two children with special needs, a new surprise—a pregnancy and the birth of our son Keller. Our first "regular education" child arrived in school only to hit his own snag by the end of first grade. A family history of dyslexia raised its ugly head for our brilliant son. (By the way, one nice thing about adopted children is that you don't curse them with family genetic faults.) And so an IEP meeting was scheduled for child number three as well. By now a pro at IEP meetings, I came prepared with my own IEP already written up, with copies for everyone in the room.

Our fourth miracle arrived on the scene in the meantime. (We needed one for the gifted-and-talented pool, didn't we?) Actually, he has not come up with a disability yet, but he's only in the second grade, so we'll give him another year or two before we start to panic.

Unbelievable? That's what I have said many times. An opportunity for learning and for creativity? You bet. For a regular education teacher with a penchant for brain research, this has been the opportunity of a lifetime (mine).

And so I write and share what I've learned from the wonderful opportunities I've been given. I write both as a special education parent and as a regular education high school teacher who has always worked with the lowest of socioeconomic students in both urban and suburban communities.

The most important thing I've learned is that sometimes you just have to laugh at yourself and your situation. You have to.

One of the other things I've learned as a teacher, parent, and brain researcher is that no two children match. Every single brain in our room is unique and special and deserves to be treated that way. No single teaching method is going to be successful with all children, because no two children are the same. So we never need to ask *why* we should differentiate instruction but rather *how* can we differentiate instruction.

And just as no two students match, no two teachers match either. Therefore one particular model will not work with all teachers. We need to look for a variety of teaching methodologies and generate ideas with enough latitude that teachers can fit them to their teaching style and their comfort level. My hope is that this book will help generate some ideas in your own creative mind that will be useful to you in your particular classroom with your particular population.

SO WHAT IS DIFFERENTIATED INSTRUCTION?

Differentiated instruction is simply providing instruction in a variety of ways to meet the needs of a variety of learners. While the term may be fairly new in education, the idea is not. As long as adults have been working with children, we've known that they learn in different fashions. More than half a century ago, educators were writing of the need for differentiation.

The term has come to the surface in a significant manner in the last couple of decades because of several major changes. First, recent research on the brain and how it learns has reinforced the idea that students do in fact learn in a variety of ways (Howard, 1994; Restak, 1995; Sylwester, 1995,

2003; Sousa, 2001; Nunley, 2002, 2003a). The elaborate pruning process we see in the brain during childhood makes it nearly statistically impossible for any two brains to match. The plasticity of the brain—the tremendous flexibility in what functions get put where and how many neurons get dedicated to particular tasks—gives physical proof of the need for a variety of teaching strategies.

Second, the past half century has seen the portion of U.S. teens enrolled in high school jump from 69 percent to 95 percent. This increase has forced the issue of differentiation. Our most significant educational change has been our shift from a selection process, whereby students of one predominant culture, ability, and learning style could attend, to a system of complete open enrollment.

Finally, differentiation has been taken on as a political agenda. Hard numbers have shown the public that traditional teaching methods are not working when applied to large numbers of the public's children. And that public is demanding change. The American dream is attached to the American school, and our society is now insisting that we accommodate everyone.

Fortunately most teachers embrace these ideas and fully support the view that all students should be successful. What trips up the process is that most high school teachers feel unprepared for their role in a differentiated classroom. And yet most teachers will find that, when they apply some simple tips and suggestions, differentiation in a high school classroom isn't just easy; it's actually a very enjoyable event. Join me as we look at some of the more common obstacles and objections among our colleagues and some very simple-to-implement solutions that make teaching—and learning—in a differentiated classroom a most exciting experience.

I Long to Return to the Good Old Days

Luke was one of the first to arrive in the classroom, as usual. Head down, backpack slung over both shoulders, he headed for his back corner of the room.

"Good morning, Luke!" I called out.

"Mmng," came the mumbled response, directed more to the floor than to me.

Poor Luke. It was obvious that school was not his "thing." Or at least general biology was not his thing. Punctual, yes, but he was a definite nonparticipant. While a part of me felt sad for him, he was not an easy child to bond with. He rarely spoke, did not participate, and slept through as much of the class as he could get away with.

While I headed toward the back of the room to visit with him that day, fully intent on trying to improve his performance in my class, the room started to fill quickly. Funny thing about a classroom: you can go from zero to forty in the space of 2½ minutes! So my excursion to see Luke was intercepted by another, more personable, character, Charlie.

"Hey, Ms. Nunley!" came the sunny shout from Charlie. "How ya doin'?"

"Hi, Charlie. I'm great. Good to see you."

More students arrived. "Well, good morning Lia." "Good morning Katy." And so started another day of third period general biology.

I was working on several student-centered classroom designs that year and using my classroom as a lab to develop what would become Layered Curriculum (Chapter 3), and my classroom was my laboratory that year. I began the class with a brief lecture to introduce a new unit concept.

Luke made a three-minute attempt to stay awake during my introductory lecture.

As soon as I finished my short lecture, I started my standard once-around-the-room quick tour to make sure everyone was working on something before I started my one-on-one assessment. I stopped at Luke's desk to wake him up and suggest a simple seatwork assignment he might like to work on today.

I stopped at Luke's desk again on my second tour to wake him up and visit for a few minutes about types of assignments he likes in other classes, thinking he might give me some insight into how to tailor assignments to his learning style. He was not a fountain of information.

I meant to stop by Luke's desk a third time because I could see he was still not engaged, but we ran out of time, and the other 38 students claimed a share of my attention as well.

"One of these days," I said to myself, "I'm going to get back there and spend some serious time with Luke. There must be something he likes to do. He must have a favorite subject, hobby, or area of interest."

That was the day I decided that Luke would be the perfect subject for a shadowing assignment I was required to do for a course I was taking. The course was in adolescent psychology, and we were asked to pick an adolescent we knew and, incognito, follow the student throughout a typical day, making behavioral observations. I would choose Luke. That would give me an opportunity to see where his strengths really were. What classes did he like? Surely he was excelling somewhere, perhaps in English class or music. I was sure there was a teacher somewhere who had a great relationship with Luke. How did he interact with friends? What teachers did he hit it off with? Perhaps I could pick up some ideas I could use to work better with Luke.

I arranged for a personal day off, secured a substitute for my classes, and got permission from all of Luke's teachers to track him through a school day.

What I discovered the day I shadowed Luke changed my view of high school teaching. It turned out Luke didn't shine anywhere. There was no class where he excelled. No teacher had a good relationship with Luke. Luke had no real friends. He moved from class to class, interacting with very few students. He sat alone at lunch. He sat in the back corner in most classrooms and kept his head down as much as he could get away with. Some teachers made attempts, as I had, to engage him. But the attempts were rather superficial, as mine had been. After all, there were 35 or so other students in the room, all needing the teacher's attention. The general belief among his teachers was that he wasn't doing well in their particular class, but they were sure, as I was, that he must be doing well somewhere else. He had to be. After all, he had perfect attendance. Luke came every day.

The truth was that no one touched Luke. He was a lost boy in a system that hides behind the security of diffusion of responsibility—the idea that there are so many people involved in a situation that we are responsible for only a tiny piece of the whole that we share.

We all know a lot of Lukes, the student we don't reach. We have at least one or two every year. We avoid guilt with the assumption that he or she is doing well elsewhere or that "someone" is reaching the child. The problem is that the large institutional high school system makes it easy for us to make these assumptions.

Add to that assumption our large, sometimes overwhelming class loads, a tradition of textbook-driven instructional methods, a shortage of opportunities to interact with colleagues to discuss particular students and coordinate efforts, and the ever increasing pressure to cover volumes of state curricula. It is little wonder that we lose many of our students at the secondary level. We lose them physically, emotionally, and socially.

Most of us know that the answer lies in some type of individualized program of instruction, but we are overwhelmed at the prospect of tailoring instruction for between 120 and 240 students. The good news is that differentiated instruction doesn't have to be hard or overwhelming. There are many things teachers can do at the high school level to help individualize instruction, thereby making school more successful for everyone—even Luke.

A DESCRIPTION OF THE ISSUE

Those of us who work in America's high schools know the resistance we feel when it comes to differentiation. There is some unspoken hope that if we drag our feet long enough, the topic will just go away. There is a belief that somehow we shouldn't have to differentiate. If the students would just shape up and try harder, they could learn through our traditional methods. We hear the conversations in the faculty room, in the hallways, and in our teacher inservices. We blame the situation on the current environment of busy parents raising undisciplined children and a school system which has taken away our authority out of increasing fear of litigation. We silently long for the good old days of school as they exist in our mental model, shaped by our own personal school days, the media, and literature.

Differentiation and *Differentiated Instruction* have been slowly creeping into the everyday vocabulary of America's classroom teachers since the early 1980s, when the National Commission on Excellence in Education released its findings on the state of our country's education system. The report, *A Nation at Risk*, furnished proof of what many classroom teachers already suspected: America's schools were not educating most of America's children.

There was public outcry over the findings in the report. While the truth was that America had never educated most of its children, the results quickly became a political agenda, and America had a change of heart. Suddenly it became important to this nation that we be successful in our attempt to educate our masses. Along with that cry for change came the mistaken belief that this was a new problem.

It came to be strongly believed that we used to educate people successfully back in the "good old days" and that what we needed to do was return to the basics of previous eras. Unfortunately that push for "back-to-the-basics" failed to bring the anticipated successful results.

Educators started to see that the basics and traditional instruction were successful, not because they were necessarily excellent ideas, but mostly because the students attending schools during that era had been hand-picked to be there. For those chosen students, we then set up a system that would cover a lot of material in a short time, and those students who could learn that way were allowed to attend. Those who could not learn that way went elsewhere.

Jack Canfield and Frank Siccone, in the preface to their book *101 Ways to Develop Student Self-Esteem and Responsibility* (1993), described a thought shared by many writers and educators:

> Our schools are in crisis. It is a crisis that has existed for decades and that persists in spite of governmental commissions, blue-ribbon panels, back-to-basics programs, alternative schools, and other attempts at reform. The problem is deeper than declining test scores, low teacher morale, student violence, drugs, and apathy. These are merely symptoms of the real issue, which is a moral one: our schools have lost their sense of mission. It is no longer clear to the educators, to the government, nor to the general public exactly what we want or need our schools to do. (p. ix)

Continuing today, educators and our educational organizations feel that our high schools have lost some sense of mission. Even a recent article by the National Association of Secondary School Principals describes the need for systemic reform in a similar way:

> To be fully committed to high school reform, we must systemically reculture and improve the high school. The historical structure and purpose of the U.S. high school are no longer adequate to serve the needs of all of the nation's youth and provide them with the skills necessary to compete in the global marketplace of the 21st century. Significant improvement is needed, but such improvement can only be attained through a substantial change in the structure and culture of the high school. (National Association of Secondary School Principals, 2005)

This sentiment, that somehow schools have lost sight of their mission, that test scores and student participation, motivation, and success were much higher back in the "good old days" when schools knew exactly what they were doing and had a defined and clear mission, is pervasive in education.

And yet this pervasive belief, while popular, is a false one. Let us take a brief look at the struggle for purpose in the history of the American high school. You may find the historical journey rather humorous. What we will find is that the arguments we hear in our faculty rooms today are the same as those voiced 200 years ago.

Schools, particularly high schools and the high school education system itself, have been struggling with their purpose and mission since the dawn of our high school system over two centuries ago.

While high school has become a reality for the masses just in our lifetime, the notion of the American high school is quite old. In fact the high school goes back to the year 1779. It was Thomas Jefferson who started our high school system that year by opening 20 secondary schools in the state of Virginia. These first high schools were not open to just anyone, of course. Only boys who could demonstrate extreme ability on a rigorous test and were considered bright in the primary grades were allowed to attend. The school lasted two years, and sometimes two or three more years were added for students considered really gifted and bright. The curriculum in these early high schools was limited to reading and studying the classics, English grammar, geography, and arithmetic.

And what was the purpose and mission of these early high schools? Simply to take the best of the best and allow them to work one-on-one with university-trained mentors to become lifelong scholars. Period. These early secondary schools were terminal programs. They did not feed the university system.

So for a brief period, it appeared that high schools had a guiding purpose—to make a few lifelong scholars who could hand down well-thought-out philosophies to help govern our nation. However, that purpose fit only two out of every 1,000 students, as that was the admission rate. Imagine what you could do today if you took your school of 1,500 students and chose the top three kids to stay. Everyone else would go home so that you could work one-on-one with this select group for the next three or four years!

This high school system grew slowly. It wasn't until 60 years later, in 1840, that a few high schools were bold enough to start admitting girls. By the mid-1800s, the public began to see a better use for tax-supported high schools, and the 150-year debate began. The goal of lifelong scholar began to be questioned. The discussion shifted to the issue of purpose, and there was mumbling that perhaps high schools should have a more practical mission.

The Industrial Revolution had increased the number of management jobs, and the cities and mill towns of New England suddenly needed trained young people to assume those positions. The existing high schools, with their high standards and clear scholarly mission, did not want to soil themselves with technical classes designed to train factory managers. So around factory towns sprang up new high schools with a new mission: To provide practical training and skills for the benefit of the community businesses and business leaders.

Both the existing and the new schools were called high schools and were tax supported, so we can understand why the public slowly forced the two institutions to merge: cost savings. But there was strong opposition to the mergers and a definite philosophical division within the high schools as to what their purpose was. The key debate was whether high schools should provide training for local businesses or educate students for the sheer value of scholarship and a classical education. (Does that argument sound familiar?)

The high school floundered with this mixed mission for the next hundred years. Despite the additional curriculum, high schools still served a very small percentage of the population. Through the 1800s very few people ever attended high school—less than 0.03 percent of the population, in fact. Schools in rural areas remained primarily scholarly, with a curriculum that focused on classic Greek and Latin. The urban, mill town high schools sought to teach a curriculum that prepared students to work in the factories. Around the turn of the twentieth century, we see a new mission added as many high schools began to see themselves as teacher preparation institutions. All of these high schools, even as late as 1900, were fairly isolated to the Midwest and New England states. The south did not have high schools until the twentieth century.

The high schools were publicly funded. Since everyone paid for them, a recurring debate raged in the early 1900s: Was the high school worth the cost? Who was benefiting from this publicly funded institution? There was little or no uniformity or purpose. No common goal. No common mission.

So over 100 years ago taxpayers were asking for some accountability from their high schools. There was outcry that they had no common mission or had lost sight of if. The debate has never ended, and the mission and purpose have become even more muddled in the twentieth century.

Although today many see the high school's main purpose as preparation for college, it wasn't until American high schools were 150 years old that colleges and universities began to see them as something that might benefit higher education. In the 1920s universities began to see high schools as possible feeder schools, in other words, a college-prep program. Accreditation programs were set up for high schools, and campaigns started.

As universities entered the mix in the 1920s, the American high school experienced its most drastic change. For the first time ever, the public began to see high school as an option for anyone. For many reasons, not the least of which was that increased high school attendance could reduce the number of people looking for work, enrollment doubled in a decade.

The timing was most unfortunate as school finances were at their worst. High school budgets were stretched. Programs and positions were cut. Curriculum was redesigned to leave the less expensive programs in place and remove the more costly ones. There was significant outcry from the media that high school was too big a burden. The public was upset at having to pay for something that benefited only a minority. One thing the public was clear on: standards were needed.

High schools were frantically trying to appease the public, raise admission standards, and redesign curriculums to somehow please both universities and local businesses. (Does this sound familiar?) Again the high school was without a well-defined purpose.

As far back as the mid-1920s, educators were writing about the need for a clear purpose for American high schools. In 1926, Henry Morrison wrote *The Practice of Teaching in the Secondary School*, one of the early books for high school teachers. In the first chapter, he described the struggle for purpose and a single vision for American high schools:

> About 1900 . . . ordinary folks in ever-increasing numbers began to plan to send their children to college. The easy-going ways which had answered for a century would no longer serve. The history of educational administration since 1890 is to a large extent a story of endless efforts to make the elementary school, the high school, and the college pull together for a common educational purpose. (p. 4)

The original purpose of the current three-tiered education system (from 1920):

- Primary School: for students to learn to read and write.
- Secondary School: for students who can THINK while reading and writing.
- Colleges and Universities: for students who can THINK independently while reading and writing.

This teaching book written 80 years ago goes on to explain quite simply the focus, goal, and purpose of public schools as they were believed to be in the 1920s. It was generally accepted that the purpose of primary school was to teach basic reading and writing skills. Then, once students had mastered reading and writing to the point that they could actually *think* while reading and writing but still needed guidance, they would move to secondary schools. If you could think while reading and writing and do so in an independent way, you were ready for college. And that became the mission of the original three-tiered American school system.

By the 1930s, enrollment numbers had grown so much that now a whopping 4 percent of the U.S. population had attended high school. This growth generated a new problem: increasing diversity. Once general enrollment in high school started to reach about 5 percent of the public, high school educators became vocal about establishing a central focus and purpose for high school. Some students were there for technical training and some to go on to college, but some were not quite ready for college when they finished high school. Teachers lamented that they could not possibly deal with this confusion of purpose and diversity of student skill levels.

The education system began to seek solutions for this multipurpose institution by making the system more complex. Perhaps the answer would lie in adding more tiers to the system. For students finishing high school unprepared for college, they would create an intermediate step. And so the junior college was born.

Figure 1.1   Growth in High School Completion Rates Through the Twentieth Century

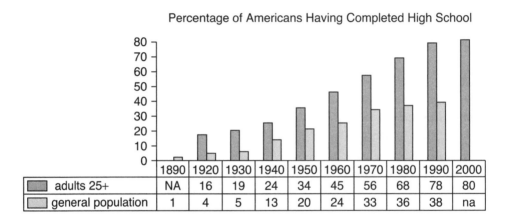

Percentage of Americans Having Completed High School

	1890	1920	1930	1940	1950	1960	1970	1980	1990	2000
adults 25+	NA	16	19	24	34	45	56	68	78	80
general population	1	4	5	13	20	24	33	36	38	na

Although high schools actually began in the 1820s as simple schools designed to be terminal institutions, they were open to only a select group of boys who excelled on rigorous exams. Those high schools were intended not to prepare the boys for college but to serve as stand-alone programs. This idea of high school continued even as late as 1890, when only 0.03 percent of the population ever attended a high school. But the twentieth century saw changes in the way the public viewed high school, and attendance rates grew rapidly. As early as 1920, the philosophy of the high school shifted. Universities started to take an interest in them as preparatory institutions and organized accrediting associations to standardize a college prep curriculum for the nation's high schools. The public began to see high schools as something that most people should attend, and by 1930 attendance had grown to 4 percent of the U.S. population. From that time, high school became more and more common, and by 1940 73 percent of teens (ages 14 through 17) were enrolled in high school, and 13 percent of the general population had graduated from high school. By 1970 94 percent of teens attended high school, and 33 percent of the general population had a high school diploma. In 1990, 38 percent of the nation had graduated from high school.

Note: Data from U.S. Census Bureau and U.S. Department of Education.

But the high school teachers were frustrated with the large spread of the skill levels of entering students. They needed an intermediate step between primary school and high school to give students with deficient skills an opportunity to catch up. And so the junior high was born. It was honestly thought that the junior high school could fix any major flaws or deficits in basic skills of students leaving primary school so that all students would now enter high school equally prepared. (I hope you are at least chuckling by now.) The most amazing part of this story is that all this outcry, frustration, and repair effort started when only 5 percent of the general population attended high school!

SOLUTION STRATEGIES

We Must Start to See That the Good Old Days Are Now

The problems we face in the philosophy of the high school are not new. There were no "good old days" of uniformity, effectiveness, and clear mission. High schools have been arguing over their mission for more than 200 years. Lest you think those "happy days" came later, perhaps when you were attending high school, let us look at what was written in the latter half of the twentieth century about funding, public support, and a united focus of vision.

In the early 1970s, educators were still lamenting the decline of public schools. Harry Good and James Teller in 1973 wrote as follows:

> In the decades since [our last edition in 1956] schools have been subjected to a two-pronged attack: first they were blamed for low academic standards, lack of rigor, and too little and the wrong kind of science and mathematics; then they were accused of ignoring the emotional and social needs of the child at the expense of his intellectual development. (p. v)

The following decade brought the same song, different verse.

> It is hard to know who the secondary schools are serving well. Dropout rates are high . . . with an even higher proportion of blacks and hispanics [sic] abandoning public schooling before graduating. College Entrance Examination Board scores have shown a steady decline . . . and college faculty lament the weak, sometimes nonexistent, academic tool skills of entering classes. There is the ever-present complaint of the lack of correspondence between the demands of high school and those of the post-school world. . . . Study panels and commissions report that secondary education generally fails to build skills for the transition from school the working world. (Wilcox, 1982, p. 1)

And in the last decade of the twentieth century, educators still sang the battle cry:

American education is in deep trouble. Most reform movements are engaged in a fruitless search for magic-bullet solutions to education's problems . . . the nation's students are caught in an education system that is sliding from mediocrity to outright failure. (Pauley, 1991, p. 197)

And so we see there never were days of old when success was found in all high schools, with all students. The rumors that there was once a time when teachers felt that the majority of their students came well prepared and ready to learn, when one teaching method fit the needs of every learner in the room, are just that—rumors.

There was never a time when the high school was not caught between the needs of the university, the needs of business, and the needs of the community. The battle has been raging for 200 years. The problems and struggles haven't changed.

The public outcry for standards and changes also continues, and perhaps has even increased. Typically, the suggested solutions from the public and political arena are things like longer school days, or more school days, or more time spent on the basic skills. But the essential question, rarely answered, is what would students do with more? More time to be unengaged? More time to be off task, more time to not fit in the classroom? More time for what?

How has this public pressure and criticism continued for so long? Probably because the community outside the school often does not see that the components and makeup of the classroom have changed while teaching methods have remained the same. The public cry is frequently to solve the problem by increasing the amount of time spent with traditional teaching methods. Initiatives by the public ask for longer school days, longer school years, more instructional time, less time on nonacademic disciplines—the "what we need here is a bigger hammer" syndrome. We push harder and harder with familiar solutions while the fundamental problems persist or even worsen. We don't need a bigger hammer. We need a different hammer. Instruction needs to be differentiated within the classroom to address the increased diversity.

What has changed, and changed dramatically, is the percentage of Americans who come through our doors. Diversity in the high school classroom isn't new; it's just grown, and grown on a scale never before seen in any nation. Very few industrialized nations make it a goal to educate their masses. We are in fact called on to do what's never been done before—get 99 percent of America's children through a one-track high school system so that they emerge prepared for a wide variety of post–high school endeavors and do it in such a fashion that our success can be measured quantitatively.

Are we up to the challenge? Absolutely!

I Thought I *Was* Differentiating

A DESCRIPTION OF THE ISSUE

If differentiated instruction means just that we are teaching using a variety of teaching strategies, then most of us certainly would consider ourselves differentiating. After all, if I present a lecture and a worksheet packet on Monday, then show a video and hand out another worksheet packet on Tuesday, and on Wednesday put the students in small groups to complete another worksheet packet, then we're ready for a whole-class review on Thursday and a test on Friday. That's differentiating, right?

Not necessarily. Differentiation means we offer a variety of instructional strategies for the same specific objective. In other words, on Monday we can lecture, but we may want to provide some other way for students to acquire the information besides listening to our lecture. And we are not really differentiating if most of our teaching activities still involve some type of worksheet or writing activity as the chief mode of processing and assessment. What about the children who really struggle with writing? They are left out of the learning on four out of the five days this week! And notice how the final assessment is the same for everyone in the class.

A frequent writer on differentiated instruction, Carol Ann Tomlinson (1995), writes:

> A class is not differentiated when assignments are the same for all learners and the adjustments consist of varying the level of difficulty of questions for certain students, grading some students harder than others, or letting students who finish early play games for enrichment. It is not appropriate to have more advanced learners do extra math problems, extra book reports, or after completing their "regular" work be given extension assignments. (p. 9)

11

So differentiated instruction doesn't mean just using a variety of teaching strategies. We must structure the actual process of learning for the needs of our students. Let us sometimes march to their tune rather than expecting all of them to march to ours. Such structuring does require a paradigm shift in classroom philosophy for most teachers.

When you differentiate your classroom, you don't differentiate just how students learn; you may sometimes need to differentiate what they learn and certainly how you assess that learning actually took place. Tomlinson (2001) writes about this very succinctly when she says that there are three learning areas that should be differentiated: content, process, and product.

Differentiated Instruction means you differentiate:

- Content
- Process
- Product

SOLUTION STRATEGIES

Be aware of differentiation at all three of these instructional levels. Are you differentiating content? You may ask, "How can I differentiate content when I'm teaching a state-mandated curriculum?" Look for areas within your standards where there is room for some student choice in content. We may need to teach about the characteristics of mammals, but does each child have to focus on the same characteristics or the same order of mammals? We may need to learn the causes of the Vietnam War, but couldn't students have some choice in a focus area? British literature is important, but aren't there enough excellent pieces that we could have student choice? Pulleys and inclines are significant machines, but couldn't students view them from a variety of situations?

As we'll see in greater detail in many of the subsequent chapters, choice is the key to differentiating your classroom. And content choice is an easy solution strategy. Stay with your standards and essential skills, but find ways students can choose categories of study so that you increase student interest. You can engage reluctant learners with choice, and you may find that later those same students are more cooperative in the areas where student choice is not an option.

The second differentiation area, process, is the one that many of us feel most comfortable differentiating. We certainly understand that there are many ways to learn vocabulary, many ways to glean the important ideas of a text, and many ways to do inquiry-based assignments. What we may not feel comfortable with, though, is having the variation going on simultaneously.

The thought of "allowing" students to opt out of my lecture because they would rather read the material in a book is a little unsettling. Besides the obvious damage to my ego that someone would find a textbook more interesting than my lecture, there is also that insidious mental question, "What will people think?" What if someone were to walk in my room and see me lecturing while five of my students were reading books rather than paying attention to my lecture, and I was not attending to that obvious infraction! The whole scenario would reflect very badly on me as a teacher. Pretty soon I'd carry the reputation of a teacher who can't control her class. The kernel of truth here is that our mental model of what a good teacher does may be the antithesis of what a differentiated classroom looks like.

You don't have to subscribe to the chaos theory of the classroom in order to differentiate the process of learning. Keep as much structure as you need. Start with small choices in how students learn. Keep objectives the same; vary the process of learning the objective. You may want to start with just two choices in seatwork, or two varieties of group projects. You can add more choices as you and your students get comfortable with multiple events in the classroom.

The third area to differentiate is the product. The product is the demonstration of the learning. This may be the assignment, the quiz, the test, the performance—whatever traditionally is "graded." Keep in mind that the goal of all your hard work is to get students to learn something; in other words, at the end of the process, students will have changed their knowledge bank, understanding, or behavior. They can write better, play with more finesse, build with greater skill, work faster, discuss a topic using more background information, and so on. So ask yourself, are there a variety of ways that students can demonstrate this? Vary your assessment. Vary the ways students can demonstrate what you asked them to learn.

Let us also remember that assessment should be done all along the way. Don't save all your assessment for the end, or you will miss some wonderful teaching moments. Subsequent chapters will focus on strategies for differentiated and along-the-way assessment. Assessments should be used frequently, not just for grades, but also for student feedback: to check for understanding and provide clarification. Use assessment as one more teaching tool. And not all assessments need to be graded and recorded in your grade book. Offer students the opportunity for frequent self-checks along the way.

PRACTICE ASSIGNMENTS FOR OVERCOMING THIS OBSTACLE

Try some of these strategies for differentiating **Content**:

Practical Solution Idea 2.1: Require "running assignments" which continue for a whole grading period and are to be done during a student's spare time. The running assignments can vary widely.

For example, a friend of mine teaches junior English. Each grading term, students have a book report due on any of the "top seller" books from her special bookshelf. She maintains a shelf of the most popular reading material. When students have any free time in class, they go back to the reading area and work on their book. It needs to be finished by the end of the term. Because the selection is limited to "bestsellers," students are more enthusiastic about the opportunity, and if they run short on time, they can find the book at a public library or a bookstore.

One of my science colleagues has a running lab project that students work on independently through the grading term. They choose their project at the start of the term from a wide variety of choices. The students use any free class time they have to work on the project. These are valuable and interesting assignments that involve such activities as growing plants, setting up habitats, and decaying foods—tasks that take too much time to do in a regular teaching unit.

Practical Solution Idea 2.2: Use interdisciplinary assignments to offer choice within an objective.

An algebra teacher in the state of Texas knows very well the skills that Texas considers essential. But the objectives leave a lot of room for creativity. In the unit on linear functions and equations, for example, two of the objectives are as follows: (1) the student can use symbols to represent unknowns and variables, and (2) the student understands that a function represents a dependence of one quantity on another. Both of these objectives can be applied to economic issues, social history issues, science issues, and even many areas of art. This teacher teams with several colleagues in the school to write interdisciplinary projects and assignments such as graphs and historical data analysis.

Try one of these strategies for differentiating **Process**:

Practical Solution Idea 2.3: List the main objective on the assignment sheet or board, but offer two or three ways that students can learn or master the objective.

For example, vocabulary is a staple in my biology class. Everyone needs to learn the vocabulary, but I give students a choice in how they do that. The objective may be that students learn the following vocabulary words: *angiosperm, gymnosperm, xylem, phloem, seedless vascular, companion cells, stoma, cuticle, meristem.*

Students can learn these by:

(a) Writing the word, the text definition, and their own definition, and then learning them.

(b) Dividing the words with a classmate, then making flashcards and quizzing each other for 20 minutes.

(c) Making flashcards with the word on the front and an illustration of the definition on the back.

The assessment remains the same: vocabulary quiz.

Practical Solution Idea 2.4: List three different ways students should be able to learn an objective. Require that on each topic they do two of the three.

Fred, a social studies teacher in Las Vegas, has this standard assignment on every unit:

Choose 2 of 3:

1. Listen to my lecture.

2. Listen to the CD of the text on the computer.

3. Read the chapter in the text.

Try one of these strategies for differentiating **Product:**

Assessment does not always have to mean formal written test. There are an infinite number of ways to measure learning. Just the word "test" is so stressful for some students that testing rarely gives us an accurate picture of their learning. Differentiate your classroom by varying the product of learning.

Practical Solution Idea 2.5: Not all assessments have to be graded and recorded in the teacher's grade book. Offer some written tests and quizzes that are self-graded, or even teacher graded, but are not recorded. The purpose is for students to receive self-feedback. Let students know that it is important for them to monitor their progress and understanding as they go along.

Practical Solution Idea 2.6: Encourage or require small-group discussion of homework. Instead of just having students hand in their completed homework assignments, assemble the students in small groups and have them (1) discuss what they have learned and what they still struggle with, and (2) get their peers' feedback on their progress. Have students pose questions or points of confusion and find a peer who can provide answers.

Practical Solution Idea 2.7: Offer a variety of ways students can present what they have learned. In addition to a formal written evaluation, have a brief conversation with your students to see what else they learned which you may not have caught with your test. Allow students to demonstrate their learning in a class or group debate. Have a group presentation of learning with murals, plays, bulletin boards, newspaper publications, video presentations, or animated tales.

I Teach the Way I Was Taught

A DESCRIPTION OF THE ISSUE

Teachers teach they way they were taught for two reasons: it is what we know, and it is what personal experience tells us works. Just as we parent the way we were parented, teachers tend to teach with the teaching style in which they were taught. Many of us, perhaps even the majority of us, came up through an education system that focused heavily on the text-book-reading-and-teacher-lecturing format. While elementary classes may have offered us some hands-on opportunities, once we entered secondary school, the overwhelming teaching technique we encountered was this traditional lecture/text format.

As college graduates, we were obviously successful with that particu-lar lecture-textbook method of instruction, so we make one of the most common and fundamental judgment errors because of it. We assume that since we were successful learning that way, everyone else should be too. Not only do we consider this to be a good way to learn; it is also one of the methods we are most comfortable with. The comfort of this traditional lecture-heavy method of teaching probably does more to maintain its use than any other factor. Add to that the fact that very little information is available about more student centered approaches to teaching, especially at the high school level, and it is little wonder that the lecture-textbook method is so pervasive.

But let's face it, that traditional classroom is rigid in style. It is geared to one type of student or at best a small range of students. Educating all the variations in culture, language, ability, and learning style has become something akin to trying to fit square pegs into round holes. Because this traditional method has not been modified to fit the variations in students,

students who want to succeed have been forced to modify their learning style to fit the template or risk failure. And failure is no longer an option in the eyes of this nation.

In addition to public opinion and philosophy changes, we now have federal mandates through the No Child Left Behind Act that require every child to be successful in school. Not three out of 1000, as it was 200 years ago, or 40 out of 100, as it was a half-century ago, or even 50 to 90 out of 100, as it was just a decade ago (numbers vary by culture and community; U.S. Government Census records). We must strive for all students to be successful.

One of the difficulties here is that it is hard to do what we've never seen done. But we must start to think differently about how classrooms operate. This task calls on our creative genius and great skill as educators. It does not require, however, that we give up our strong belief that education through the written and spoken word is important.

No one is going to argue over the genuine value in a lecture-textbook system based on reading, writing, and listening. Our culture places a high value on words, and justifiably so. Reading and writing are at the top of the list of skills emphasized and taught in schools. We value them so highly because we see the written word as one of the most powerful ways to change the world. "The pen is mightier than the sword" is the battle cry of a civilized people.

However, much research has been published showing us that a teacher-centered, didactic classroom with a heavy emphasis on lecture, textbooks, and video is just not conducive to long-term learning or to an increased ability to transfer that knowledge to other situations (Blumenfeld et al., 1991; Atwater, 1995; Keegan, 1995; Harris, 1995; Renyi, 1993; Ryan, et al., 1998; Reeve, Bolt, & Cai, 1999; Kern, et al., 2001; Nunley, 1996, 2002; Vansteenkiste et al., 2004).

SOLUTION STRATEGIES

Let us start on the journey for change by looking at our own mental models of learning. Keep in mind that you were successful in school because your learning style somewhat matched the teaching style of your school. You went on to college and continued to be successful because college also matched that learning style. No offense, but you and I are the exception, not the rule. For political correctness, we may call ourselves the "statistically infrequent." Most people do not learn that way. If they did, most people would excel in high school and graduate from college.

Exposure to and support for a variety of teaching methods is the way to overcome this very real obstacle. Teachers are willing to try new methodology if they are properly trained and supported (Hargreaves & Gray, 1983; Sparks, 1988; Feiman-Nemser et al., 1989; Grossman, 1990; Jones & Vesilind, 1996; Fang, 1996; Torff, 2003; National Reading Panel,

2000). Unfortunately there has not been much in the literature or in our teacher training courses in the way of student centered models for the high school teacher. Don't be afraid to borrow from other arenas. Some of my best classroom instructional strategies have been borrowed from elementary teachers and from sources outside public education. With some modification, as we'll see in later chapters, they make fabulous additions to the high school classroom.

Teachers need ideas and collegial cooperation for building a stockpile of instructional strategies. Work with teams of teachers and colleagues in your building and your school district to share ideas, brainstorm, or make a concerted effort to expose yourself to nontraditional methods. This could be done as in-house professional development or as a continuing education project.

PRACTICE ASSIGNMENTS FOR OVERCOMING THIS OBSTACLE

Find a group of interested teachers and start an independent study group to learn about alternative teaching and learning methodologies. Your study will take you to other areas and institutions to gather information. Bring those ideas back to your group and share them. Look for ways they can be modified to fit the high school setting.

Try one or more of these assignments to help expose yourself to a variety of teaching and learning methods.

Practical Solution Idea 3.1: Purposely expose yourself to teaching and learning methodology that may be foreign to you.

Seek out and examine learning environments that traditionally have had little or no appeal to you but apparently appeal to other types of learners. You are looking for successful educational environments that do not cater to the traditional lecture-textbook-oriented learner. Either actually visit these places or brainstorm in a small-group setting to discover what you know already about how these programs operate. What types of learners do they attract? What kinds of methodologies do they use? Why do you think they use the teaching methodologies that they do?

Places you may want to visit would include:

- Technology programs. Visit vocational classes or schools. Traditionally their courses accomplish student learning using alternative methods. Note the amount of teacher-directed versus student-directed learning that goes on. Watch for student engagement. Watch for successful learning.
- Adult and community education programs. Take a community education course or visit a class. Again, many of these courses are designed to meet the learning needs of a wide variety of learners seeking to

learn a skill. Take note of the teaching methods used and the amount of teacher-led versus student centered time.

- Alternative education programs. These schools and programs specifically target students who have not been successful in more traditional settings. How are these classes different? What strategies are they using that are proving to be successful for their learners?
- Other nontraditional educational and training institutions, such as driving schools, corporate training programs, distance education, and trade schools.

The purpose of these visits is to simply increase your exposure to something other than what you've experienced in your life. If you've seen little more than traditional lecture-textbook, teacher-centered instruction, it is nearly impossible to expect you to teach any other way.

Practical Solution Idea 3.2: Go to the source.

Go on a scavenger hunt to find adults who may not have been particularly successful during their school days but are very successful now. Interview them informally to find out how they learn best. Ask what it was about school that they found difficult. What was different about their recent learning success? Let me give you a couple of examples I discovered when I did this very investigation.

> Andy is a very intelligent environmental engineer from a seacoast town in New England. Today he is a successful business owner and a well-respected consultant for governments around the world. But Andy admits he was not a very good high school student. "Looking back on it, I think I really just didn't want to be told what to do," he relates. "It wasn't until I was running my own show either in graduate school or in my own business that I really started to see success."

Andy apparently likes feeling that he is captain of his own ship. Until he could feel some real control over the direction and pace of his life, he was not successful. As a student Andy would probably benefit from a classroom that offered choice—both in how he learned and in what areas to focus on.

> Margaret is a clinical psychologist in private practice. In high school, she recalls, she was not a particularly good student. "I think I was always rather bright and intelligent, but just didn't have a focus. I was actually somewhat of a behavior problem. I only went on to college because my parents insisted. It was lucky they did. I finally found real meaning and a purpose for learning when I got most of the way through my undergraduate work. Once I had an opportunity to apply what I was learning to real situations, I became a motivated student."

Margaret would probably have benefited more from a high school that offered some of the reading motivation strategies we'll look at in Chapter 8. Some hands-on activities before reading and more social interaction opportunities to share what she was learning would have helped her get more out of high school.

Fortunately these are individuals who, although they struggled in high school, managed to hang on, discovered how they could truly learn, and now lead rather successful lives. What of the large number of students who never quite discover the gifts they have hidden inside?

Practical Solution Idea 3.3: Brainstorm outside the box.

This is a small-group activity. Gather together a few colleagues, preferably including some who are not in your teaching discipline.

- Choose one or two lesson objectives that you might teach in your classroom next week.
- Now brainstorm: How would you teach these objectives if there were no books, pencils, or paper?

Because it is tempting to state the obvious, which is that if we had no books we would lecture more, we will add an additional challenge. What if we had no books and most of our learners were limited in their ability to understand the spoken word, because of either a language barrier or a physical limitation? Now we're getting into some creative solution strategies.

- Actually write the ideas down. Turn them into assignment choices for the objectives.
- You may want to add even more challenges, such as what if we had no books and no photocopy machine. Now what?
- Keep brainstorming until you get a good number of lesson plan ideas that would teach your content in nontraditional ways.
- Now act on your ideas and really offer some of those assignments to your students.

For example, I might have the following as a teaching objective: *Students will learn the various shapes and arrangements of bacteria.* For this objective I could come up with the following nontraditional lesson ideas:

- Do some small-group lessons using modeling clay. Have the students make various designs of bacteria shapes and arrangements using modeling clay.
- Have students make a three-dimensional bulletin board display showing the shapes and arrangements.
- Have students construct a model game or set in which the pieces can be placed in various arrangements.

Practical Solution Idea 3.4: Build a list of alternative teaching activities.

You'll find through your brainstorming with colleagues that you can create a huge list of nontraditional learning activity ideas. Here are some ideas to help you get started.

- Allow students to demonstrate their learning using a pamphlet, brochure, or newsletter.
- Add some art supplies to an area of your room and allow students to use them.
- Establish an area of your room to display student-designed work.
- Buy several pieces of poster board, cut each piece into quarters, and have students make posters summarizing the key points of a lecture.
- Allow students to design the bulletin boards in your room. Each board should
  - teach one or more concepts to their classmates.
  - involve the class in a "Unit Newspaper" pertaining to one unit of study, such as The Holocaust, The Plant Kingdom, *The Adventures of Huckleberry Finn*, or Fractions and Percentages. Students are responsible for various articles and sections (news, classified ads, display ads, layout, editing, op/ed section, etc.). Publish the newspaper so that everyone gets a copy.
- Carry on a debate as a mock trial.
- Have students design ads for concepts.
- Put a lecture on audiotape and offer it as an option.
- Have students prepare a lecture and teach a concept to a small group of peers.
- Have students make murals, timelines, or other large-scale visuals.
- Make a magazine on the topic, either alone or in small groups, so that each student has a job.
- Offer small, live lectures to small groups of students in a corner of your room while other students work on something else.
- Have students search online and make an annotated bibliography of the Web sites they discover that pertain to the topic.
- Create and play board games that teach concepts.

I Don't Know How

A DESCRIPTION OF THE ISSUE

One of the biggest hurdles to differentiation is just knowing where to start. There are very few models designed for the high school classroom. It is for this very reason that I developed Layered Curriculum. Using my own classroom as a laboratory, I experimented with a variety of teaching strategies and a combination of designs to find something that would actually work in a high school classroom. It was apparent that much of what was going on in my public high school, and more specifically in my classroom, wasn't working for a significant number of students. I wanted something that would meet the needs of a very wide range of abilities and learning styles and yet be manageable for me as a teacher and encourage students to work at their maximum ability.

Like most teachers, I started out teaching in a rather traditional high school setting. Teachers in my school and especially in my department relied heavily on lecture and textbooks for instruction. Most teachers used only one textbook for their classes and used the publisher-provided ancillary materials, such as worksheets and study guides, as their sole teaching materials. Science lab activities were also generated from the textbook, with little or no original lab work designed and implemented by students.

Despite the very wide variety of abilities, cultures, and learning styles in our diverse population, only one curriculum implementation was used to serve all students. No provision was made for learning modalities, reading ability, or cultural perspective. Because teachers had the freedom to implement the curriculum as they chose, the programs were generally teacher-centered and teacher-driven, with few choices available to match the students' individual needs.

Because of all these factors, students showed a genuine lack of interest in the curriculum. Truancy rates at my school were high. Many students were not successful. Time on task was very low, and students did not feel they had any control or choice in their instructional plan. A survey was conducted to get student and faculty views on instructional strategies and student engagement. The results were that while most teachers would like to offer other teaching strategies, they still spent the majority of class time engaged in teacher-centered lectures and textbook activities. Students responded that they were expected to spend about 70 percent of their class time either reading out of a text or listening to a lecture. Off-task behavior in classrooms was as high as 75 percent, however. In other words, at any given time, three out of four students in any classroom were doing something other than what was designated as the learning activity. Not surprisingly, failure rates were high. Something had to be done.

While some failures were due to excessive truancy, there were many other causes, and many of these causes were the same things that were producing the off-task behavior: limited English skills, low reading ability, and a general lack of interest in the class activity.

It was in this very teacher-centered environment that I began to experiment with alternate ways of setting up my classroom and delivering instruction. My goals were to increase student involvement and engagement and decrease the unacceptable failure rate.

SOLUTION STRATEGIES

The Easiest Road to Differentiation Is Student Choice

I found that I, like most teachers, divided a typical class period into two sections: part one included some type of whole-class instruction, and part two involved some type of independent seat work. For example, I usually started each class period out with a lecture. I would stand at the front and introduce a topic to the students as a whole. That took half to most of the class period. The second part of the lesson involved students' doing some type of work, such as answering questions from the text, completing a worksheet packet, or carrying out a small-group activity or lab. If my lecture took most of the period, this independent work might take the form of a homework assignment.

So the most obvious place to start differentiating was in the independent seatwork. This way I could still keep my class lecture, which I felt was very important for a number of reasons, but I could allow some variety in the seatwork. And so I began offering students a choice in their independent work. Sometimes it was a choice between bookwork and worksheets. Sometimes it was a choice in labs or group work versus solo work. Once I got started, I found that having these choices was actually fun for both the students and me. I enjoyed the challenge of coming up with variations in the seatwork. I learned a lot by watching what students chose. Sometimes I would offer a rather standard type of assignment and discover that no one chose it! Those moments were quite insightful.

As I went along, the choices for independent work got more varied and creative. Sometimes I could think of three or four different assignments that would teach the same objective. The list got rather complicated, so I started writing all the options down for the week, by day, and gave that menu of planned options to the students ahead of time. Now they could look ahead and plan what types of activities they might want to work on as the unit progressed.

Add a Second Piece: Accountability

After we had a fairly smooth-running class designed around these two pieces—my teacher-centered whole-class instruction, followed by their choice in independent seatwork, practice, and elaboration—I found a need to increase the accountability in the room. As has occurred to many of us in education, just "doing" an assignment does not necessarily mean students have learned much from the assignment. Nor does this "doing" give us any indication of whether mastery has occurred or whether the students need more practice or a review. Awarding credit for "doing" assignments has been one of the most vulnerable holes in our traditional education system. By awarding points for merely doing work, we've made the unspoken assumption that learning has occurred, but as most of us know, that isn't necessarily the case.

The public scratches their head in wonder as to how students can pass through 12 years of schooling and come out at the other end sometimes still very ignorant. But educators know very well how that can happen. We don't have a learning-accountability system built into our traditional grading schema. With the exception of tests, exams, and quizzes, students are often given point credit for work with no accounting of whether or not they have learned or need more practice or even whether they are in fact the author of the work they turn in. This problem was created because a grading scheme oftentimes awards so many points for this no-accountability work that it overrides the points awarded to the accountability assignments such as tests and quizzes. Let me illustrate my point.

Walter Leilana turns in every homework assignment given in his earth science class. He comes each day, works on class work, and is punctual with all those assignments as well. Walter struggles with school and is a rather reluctant learner but has learned how to "play the game." He has a lot of friends and is a very sociable person, which gets him a lot of help on his assignments. Often the work he does himself is very little and of poor quality, but he partners up with the right people before turning things in. While Walter never does very well on tests, they count for only 20 percent of his grade, so Walter actually manages to get a C+ in earth science.

Berna Washington is a very bright student who is often bored in earth science because much of the material is a repeat of what she gleaned from her science classes in middle school. She loves science and spends a tremendous amount of time watching science documentaries on television and remembers nearly everything she has ever read on the topic. She doesn't have to work hard on earth science and actually prefers not to as she finds the assignments boring and a waste of time. She spends most of her homework time on more challenging subjects. Consequently she doesn't turn in a lot of her homework assignments and has quite a few "no grades," despite the fact that she makes rather high marks on all her tests. Because she does so few homework assignments, her class work is poor, and the exams count for only 20 percent of the grade, her course grade suffers. Berna ends up with a B- for her grade in earth science.

Berna and Walter have similar grades in earth science, a C+ and a B–. Both of these students have "passed" earth science, and both have grades that would not necessarily worry their counselors, teachers, or parents. On the transcript, they look fairly good: not excellent, but average. Outsiders viewing the grades would assume Berna and Walter know roughly the same amount about earth science. The reality is that there is a great deal of difference between what these two students know, how they function, and where they need to go now in terms of their science education. But you can't see that from a grade. Unfortunately that's all most of us have to look at when making judgments about guidance, school success, and student achievement. So what's wrong with the system? There's no accountability at the day-to-day level.

Therefore I needed to add another component to my model: accountability. Points were now going to be awarded partly or wholly for what was learned, not on what was completed on paper. I discovered that with a 30-second discussion, I could assess whether students learned or not. If you choose the end-of-the-chapter question assignment, I as the teacher could just choose one of those questions at random and ask you about it. If you could answer it, you would get the points for the whole assignment. Too harsh? Then perhaps I'd ask you two questions, each worth half the points of the assignment. That sounded better. If you did a worksheet, could you explain something from the worksheet to me quickly? If you watched a video, could you summarize what you thought were the main points? If you did vocabulary flash cards, could I pick one or two of them at random and have you define those terms in your own words?

Eureka: accountability! It no longer mattered what was down on the student's paper, or for that matter whether anything was down on paper. What mattered was, *did learning occur*? If you could watch the video and give me a really good 60-second summary of the main points, including some reflection, I found that much more productive than a piece of paper where you wrote a few things down once in awhile while watching the movie.

If a student wanted to read the text chapter, look over the end-of-chapter questions, and be prepared to answer any of them at random, face-to-face, that would be much more telling to me than paperwork of copied text passages.

This was no small shift from the students' perspective. Imagine if points in school were awarded only for learning and not for how you got to that point? It was a different world for them. Many were angry. I had changed the rules. "I did it, doesn't that count?" and "Well, I don't know—it's right there, though, on my paper" suddenly were worthless statements. The statements had to be replaced with "Here's what I learned" or "Wait, I have to look over this and study a bit" and even the exclamation, "You mean I don't have to write it all out? Wow!"

This required plain, easy-to-understand rubrics, or grading criteria, for the students. They had to know ahead of time how points would be awarded so that they would be prepared. Much to my delight, I found two wonderful teacher advantages to this approach: First, the rubrics could be written rather generically so that they fit any lesson topic (after all, vocabulary flash cards are vocabulary flash cards whether they are for genetics, bacteria, or mammals). The second big plus was that all this class discussion cut down on the amount of paperwork I was grading at home. Yes, class time was a busy time for me. I was circulating, assessing, and individualizing the instruction as needed, and at the end of the school day I was exhausted. But I also was finished! There wasn't much to take home because it was graded during the day. This was a nice trade-off.

The Final Piece: Encourage Higher-Level Thinking

Things were running smoothly after some practice. Students had choice, I had my opportunities for whole-class instruction (my lectures), and students were actually thinking their way through assignments because they knew they had to learn something in order to gain any points. My classroom was a much less stressful environment than it once was. But something was still missing. I was not assured that my students would learn to think at more and more complex levels. I wanted to make sure that students were encouraged to think and process information at all levels described in Bloom's Taxonomy. Sure, they had lots of opportunity to gather new information on a topic, but they also needed to play around with the new ideas, apply them to previously learned information, manipulate the ideas, or compare them to other ideas, and they needed to do the type of thinking essential to adult life: critical thinking.

And so the final piece of Layered Curriculum was added: the layers. Could I require students to think more complexly in order to improve their grade? What if I tied the actual letter grade to the elaboration of study? Looking at Bloom's Taxonomy, I could see that the types of learning or thinking could easily be divided into three blocks or, as I thought of them, three layers. The bottom layer dealt with adding to one's bank of knowledge, or what I casually thought of as "trivial pursuit." The middle layer deals with things like compare and contrast, apply, demonstrate, hook to prior knowledge, or what I casually thought of as "play around with it." The top layer deals with critical thinking, synthesis, and evaluation, or what I casually thought of as "voting."

LAYERED CURRICULUM™: a teaching model that divides the learning process into three layers based on the complexity of the student's thought process.

Layered Curriculum™ asks students at each layer to:

C Layer: Gather information

B Layer: Apply or manipulate that information

A Layer: Critically evaluate an issue

So there were the three layers to Layered Curriculum. I would start by asking students to gather information, and then ask them to play around with that new information and finally to critically analyze an issue on the topic, as a voter might do. The layers were then named C layer, B layer, and A layer because the letter grade the students would earn would be based on the complexity of their thinking. Now a letter grade earned in my class had some consistent meaning: A student who earned an A was one who could gather information, manipulate that information, and critically evaluate the topic with some level of proficiency and accountability.

Putting a unit into a Layered Curriculum format was fairly simple. I just took what I wanted the students to learn and divided it into the three layers: basic knowledge, connections to previous information, and a critical evaluation of real-world issues. I offered students a choice of objectives where I could. I still dedicated a good part of my class period as whole-class instruction and awarded points to students for listening to my lecture and taking lecture notes. I allowed students the option of working quietly on another unit assignment if they did not want to listen to the lecture—although nearly all of them chose to listen to the lecture every day. I required some type of accountability to earn points on most assignments. The model worked beautifully.

Layered Curriculum works well in a wide variety of subjects and grade levels. Because of its flexibility, it is one of the easiest ways to differentiate a high school classroom. Teachers can shift emphasis among layers based on the needs of their subject. Whole-class direct instruction can be used for some or nearly all of the work. Student choice can be added where possible. You can start slow and small, with a tremendous amount of structure and teacher control, and work into more variety and more layers as you and your students gain more comfort and feelings of self-efficacy and confidence. It's very adaptable. (For more information, see Nunley, 2004, or http://help4teachers.com.)

PRACTICE ASSIGNMENTS FOR OVERCOMING THIS OBSTACLE

Try building a unit of Layered Curriculum. Take what you want students to know and divide it into the three layers.

What basic new information do you want them to learn? How can they apply or connect that new information to prior knowledge or other information, and what topics are currently being debated in the real world that relate to this subject?

Practical Solution Idea 4.1: Write a variety of ways students might learn your C-layer objectives.

Offer students two or three choices in how students can learn those objectives. You may not be able to offer choices for every single objective, but look for places where you can offer some choice.

Practical Solution Idea 4.2: Write down your B-layer ideas.

Offer two or three ways students can apply their new knowledge or demonstrate it or show some mastery of it. Interdisciplinary assignments work great in this layer.

An example of a B-layer assignment might be, Watch the game Sunday (Superbowl, Red Sox, Lakers, etc.). Write the next day's sports column. Include at least three graphs and two statistical analyses.

Thomas Armstrong (1999), in *7 Kinds of Smart*, gives many examples of mind activities for teachers to use to generate ideas for lesson planning. Can you learn math musically? Can you study astronomy through art? Visualization, imaginary games, and musical challenges all can start your creative thinking. Find ways to help students find their hidden skills and strengthen their obvious skills.

Practical Solution Idea 4.3: Discover your A-layer issues.

Brainstorm with colleagues to find some current events for A-layer work. It is important to get ideas from colleagues or other people outside your field or discipline. They frequently come up with the most creative A-layer, real-world issues and questions. Any time I've been stumped for an A-layer assignment, I check with teaching colleagues or peers outside the field of education.

A-layer questions are real-world issues that may have no objectively right or wrong answer as they involve value judgments. They are issues that people are voting on and debating. They are issues about which you can find research to support more than one view. Examples are such questions as the following: Are pesticides on crops bad for us? Who is the better actor? When is it genocide and when is it a civil war? Should we require exit exams for graduation from high school? Does the school cafeteria serve a balanced meal? (For more information see Nunley, 2003, 2004.)

Worksheet for Designing a Layered Curriculum Unit

Unit Title: _____

C layer **What BASIC new knowledge do I need them to know/learn?**	Objectives:	Some assignment choices for each objective:
B layer **How can they apply this new information to previous information?** **Apply, compare, manipulate, demonstrate**	Objectives:	Some assignment choices:
A layer **What debatable issue in the real world deals with this topic?** **Current events, debates, leadership decisions**	Objectives:	Some assignment choices:
Accountability ideas: **Oral defense, homework, group think/ discuss, quizzes, partner share**		

EXAMPLE OF A LAYERED CURRICULUM UNIT

Bacteria (Kingdom Monera)

NAME _____   DUE DATE _____   Points possible: 100

C Layer: Section I—Basic Understanding (65 points maximum)

1. Take notes from daily presentations. (5 pts/day. MUST BE PRESENT) 1 2 3 4 5

2. Watch the DVD on bacteria. Take notes. Include information on bacteria shape and arrangement and ways to prevent bacteria growth. (15 points)

3. Using materials of your choice, make a three-dimensional model of a prokaryotic cell. (10 points)

4. Make 15 vocabulary flash cards using the vocabulary terms from this unit. Be able to define the terms IN YOUR OWN WORDS. (10 points)

5. Read Chapter 20 in HBJ. Be able to answer all the "Reviewing the Section" questions. (15 points)

6. Using construction paper and plain paper, make a 10-page children's book on 10 ways to prevent bacterial infections. Illustrate your book. (15 points)

7. Answer question 15–20 on page 312 of the HBJ book. (10 points)

8. Write two paragraphs, one on ways bacteria are helpful to humans and one on ways bacteria are harmful to humans. This MUST be done in a language other than English. (10 points)

9. Pass a quiz on the shapes and arrangements of bacteria. (10 points)

10. Research three types of bacterial infection: botulism, tetanus, and strep throat. Write a small, half-page report on each. List your sources of information. (15 points)

B Layer: Section II—Labs (15 points each) Choose one. These must be done in class!

1. Which surface in the school contains the most bacteria? Which the least? Using a plate with agar, swab and streak between 5 and 7 sources of bacteria around the school. Describe your colonies using the correct terms. Compare and contrast them.

2. Does hand washing reduce bacteria numbers? Prove your hypothesis using fingerprints and a plate with agar.

3. Do current face cleansers reduce bacteria present on the face? Use a plate with agar, face cleansers, and the *Staphylococcus epidermidis* from the tip of your nose. Describe the colonies.

A Layer: Section III—Use an A-Layer Assignment sheet to analyze one of these issues. (20 points)

1. What issues are we currently facing due to the overuse of antibiotics?

2. Would a campaign to encourage hand washing reduce the rate of illness at our school?

3. What role should government play in making our meat safe to eat?

Grading Scale: 86+ = A, 71–85 = B, 56–70 = C, 40–55 = D

NOTE: You will have a 50-point exam on this unit on _____.

(More sample units are available at http://help4teachers.com.)

I Have Too Much Content to Cover

THE NORTH WIND AND THE SUN—*AN AESOP'S FABLE*

The North Wind and the Sun disputed as to which was the most powerful, and agreed that he should be declared the victor who could first strip a wayfaring man of his clothes.

The North Wind first tried his power and blew with all his might, but the keener his blasts, the closer the Traveler wrapped his cloak around him, until at last, resigning all hope of victory, the Wind called upon the Sun to see what he could do.

The Sun suddenly shone out with all his warmth. The Traveler no sooner felt his genial rays than he took off one garment after another, and at last, fairly overcome with heat, undressed and bathed in a stream that lay in his path.

—Persuasion and Choice Are Better Than Force

A DESCRIPTION OF THE ISSUE

The fastest way to cover a lot of material is to lecture on the topic or give students a textbook and have them read it outside class. Few would argue that this is in fact the quickest way to get a lot "covered." As most of us have discovered, however, covering material does not necessarily mean you have taught it. Or to be more accurate, it doesn't mean students have learned it.

I actually had a teacher ask me something similar regarding my very student centered classroom. Her question was "Kathie, do you ever do any teaching, or are you just a facilitator?"

Goodness, I always thought I was teaching! I knew of course what she was really asking, and that was whether I did any whole-class instruction or lecture. But the question reminded me that as educators we often associate those activities with teaching when the truth is that if my students are learning in my classroom, regardless of how that occurs, then I am in fact teaching. The stand-and-deliver teaching methodology is so ingrained in our profession that we often define our professional success and expertise by it.

But let's see if we can start to change the way we define our view of a successful classroom teacher. We can go back more than a hundred years to get some sound advice on what our role is as teacher. One of the early pioneers in public school education, Edward Sheldon, attempted in the late 1800s to supply teachers with a true purpose: "The true idea of school education is not so much to impart knowledge as to prepare the mind to acquire knowledge and to convey it to others" (Good & Teller, 1973, p. 204).

Not a bad mission. The world today obviously changes at a much faster pace than it did in the 1800s, and so we see an even greater need for us to prepare students to learn how to learn. We need to focus on helping students be proficient at learning and integrating new information rather than simply filling their heads with a lot of isolated, rote, and unrelated information.

Today's education experts put an even greater emphasis on teaching the process of learning rather than the content (Vansteenkiste et al., 2004; Cutts & Moseley, 1960; Deci & Ryan, 1985). Emphasis should be placed on integration and application of ideas rather than simple recall. In his recent book *A Mind at a Time*, Mel Levine (2002) called for this shift:

> In devising student examinations, teachers should strive for a good balance between understanding and remembering. Tests should not reward pure recall. In secondary school, in particular, students ought to be allowed to bring several pages of their own notes. (p. 118)

The old debate continues in education over whether we should cover lots of material at a very shallow level or cover less material but to a greater extent to allow for deeper understanding. Increasingly teachers are asked to cover more and more content, which forces us to spend less and less time on each topic, and thus students never look at anything very deeply.

SOLUTION STRATEGIES

First and foremost, let your passion show. What is important is not so much that you share your knowledge with students as that you share your passion for your subject with them. Paint with broad strokes so that students come to see the bigger picture of your subject. It's not so important that students know that Faulkner is good literature but why Faulkner is good literature and how to tell good literature from bad. It's not important that they know the intricacies of DNA structure but rather what makes DNA so important in our lives and how certain future public decisions could be so dangerous.

We aren't preparing students for today but for tomorrow. The truth is that most of the jobs and job skills involved in our students' future do not even exist today. Look at the job skills we use in our profession. The personal computer, the Internet, electronic grading programs, remote controls, DVD players, video cameras, whiteboards, palm pilots, and electronic ancillary text materials. These are things many of us were never instructed in as students. In fact much of this technology did not even exist when we began our teaching profession. We had to learn how to integrate it and how to judge its usefulness on the job. We may just this year be evaluating some new technology.

Try to keep in mind that you are preparing your students to apply the key ideas of your discipline to future issues, technologies, and problems. They need to have the significant facts and processes but also the ability to apply them to other situations that may arise.

REALIZE YOU CAN'T LECTURE FAST ENOUGH

If you've been following all the research that's surfaced recently about the new dynamic brains created by our video-electronic era, then you realize educators are right in the muck of the situation. One of the brain areas that has changed the most due to all the video stimulation given children today is an area known as the reticular activating system, or sometimes called the reticular formation. This primitive area in the base of the brain has several jobs, but its big job is to focus attention. This is the area that takes all the incoming stimulation and chooses the one piece that will gain our attention. We can focus our attention on only one item at a time, regardless of how much we like to multitask. Attention is a one-item vessel. There are several things that will catch or help focus attention, but the big three are physical need, novelty, and self-made choices.

The need for novelty has changed. Ask any teacher and we'll tell you that each year we feel an increased need to put on a dog and pony show in front of the class in order to maintain the students' attention. We are not imagining this. It is the result of the new dynamic reticular formation areas of the brain. The brains of this generation's children can pick up and process new information at incredible speeds. You can see this in the video and computer games they play. You can see it in the music videos they watch and in any animated production. Scenes change at incredible speeds. Video and other visual electronics have trained these new brains to process fast, real fast. The down side of course comes when you try to educate these brains in traditional classrooms, where the teaching methodology hasn't changed in 200 years. A lecture seems incredibly slow to these young brains. They are easily bored. They have a difficult time maintaining attention (Christakis et al., 2004; Tervaniemi & Hugdahl, 2003).

One of the simplest ways to solve this issue is to focus on the third item in the list of attention motivators above: the perception of self-made choices. Let students perceive they are choosing some of the learning activities. Let them pace themselves. Let them gather and absorb information at a pace they control. The new reticular formation has an easier time in a more student centered classroom than in a traditional lecture presentation.

As was also mentioned earlier, educational research continues to demonstrate that student centered classrooms increase retention and a student's ability to later apply learned information. In fact student centered classrooms reduce destructive behavior, reduce dropout rates, increase time on task, and increase students' perceived pleasure in learning. Student centered approaches still allow for covering the core curriculum, but they allow students to fill out that core in their own unique fashion (Benware & Deci, 1984; Stainback & Stainback, 1992; Flink et al., 1992; Patrick, Skinner, & Connell, 1993; Boggiano, et al., 1993; Valleran, Fortier, & Guay, 1997; Reeve, Bolt, & Cai, 1999; Kern et al., 2001; Lodewyk & Winne, 2005; Walls & Little, 2005).

Even content-heavy classes can allow for much student choice and control. While I found success in differentiating my general biology classroom, I struggled for some time in differentiating my advanced placement classes. There was so much content, and it all had to be covered. I finally discovered that these classes could be built on a traditional foundation of lectures and textbook readings but that adding more application and critical thinking assignments and opportunities also allowed me opportunities to differentiate the curriculum.

Student centered classrooms also free the teacher's time for more serious and in-depth small-group instruction, which can significantly improve student understanding. While the students are working, the teacher can move around the classroom to check for individual problems, clarify issues, and make individual assessments.

PRACTICE ASSIGNMENTS FOR OVERCOMING THIS OBSTACLE

Practical Solution Idea 5.1: Cover your usual content in a class lecture, but offer students two or three choices for how they want to play with, practice, or apply that information.

Most of us, regardless of the subject we teach, use the two-part system in our class periods. Part one involves some type of whole-class instruction. Whether that is some kind of lecture, a whole-class discussion, a story to be read, or a class demonstration, video, or chalk talk, most of us begin each class by offering something to the group of students as a whole. We introduce the day's topic. We follow that with some type of seatwork. This is the second part of the class, often finished at home. Here is where we ask students to practice what we have just introduced or to manipulate the concepts or apply what we've discussed.

You can maintain this format, but when you get to the seatwork (or homework) portion, simply offer students a choice in how they want to do that work.

One of the pioneers and most prolific writers in the research on the intrinsic motivating benefits of student centered classrooms, Edward Deci (1995), wrote as follows:

> The main thing about meaningful choice is that it engenders willingness. It encourages people to fully endorse what they are doing; it pulls them into the activity and allows them to feel a greater sense of volition; it decreases their alienation. When you provide people choice, it leaves them feeling as if you are responsive to them as individuals. And providing choice may very well lead to better, or more workable, solutions than the ones you would have imposed. (p. 34)

Practical Solution Idea 5.2: Have students supplement the information gleaned from the textbook with either supporting or conflicting information from a different text.

Use a variety of textbooks in your classroom. You can collect these from other teachers in your building or from the district central office or warehouse. Sample copies of texts you are previewing for adoption can be added to your classroom supply. Try to gather texts with varying viewpoints, writing styles, and readability levels.

Students need to start viewing a textbook as just one of several places they can get information. Let them examine opposing viewpoints in texts. Find a text that is several decades old and examine how times and attitudes may affect the way a textbook presents a particular issue.

Practical Solution Idea 5.3: Offer choice in the homework assignments.

If you find it difficult to move away from whole-class assignments for the vast majority of your class period, try to differentiate the way students practice the skill or offer a variety of ways they can apply or manipulate that information. Look for alternate ways of ways homework can be done. Can you vary the number of problems to be worked? Can you add variety to the topic of application? While your students may all be required to listen to your lecture or read from your adopted textbook, they can all find individual and unique ideas from their personal lives to apply the concepts to.

I'm Good at Lecturing

A DESCRIPTION OF THE ISSUE

The vast majority of high school teachers use lecture as the mainstay of their instruction. High school budgets easily support the perpetuation of this lecture-textbook mode with ample allocation of funds for textbooks. Even the physical classroom design supports this lecture-heavy, teacher-centered approach, and most of us feel confident in our ability to lecture. In a survey of high school teachers, the most frequently reported reason given for why we lecture is self-efficacy. We feel we are good at it and that our lectures are engaging and worthwhile. To move away from this perceived successful strategy leaves a teacher feeling uneasy and perhaps even a little frightened.

But there is no shortage of reasons and research to indicate high schools should be replacing or supplementing some of the traditional lecture-textbook method with alternative instructional strategies. This does not mean that we need to give up this comfortable pedagogy, but we need to look for additional strategies to increase the population of successful learners in our classroom.

While a homogeneous classroom may be very comfortable for the teacher, one of the strongest arguments against a primarily lecture-based class in high school is that it promotes ability grouping and segregates special needs students (Manning & Lucking, 1990; Willis, 1995). Some teachers in fact use this lecture-heavy format as a way to maintain a segregated classroom. By offering only this one teaching strategy, you easily assure yourself a school-wide reputation that encourages only those traditionally successful students to enroll. This population is often viewed as the most desirable student population as they learn in traditional ways. They belong to those groups known as high ability, bright, college bound, or gifted.

A large majority of high school teachers feel that students learn best when grouped by ability. There's no question that grouping students makes the teacher's job easier. If we are dependent on lecture-textbook instruction, it is easier to teach to a group of students with little variation in ability level so that we can aim the text and our lectures to a common group. And despite research to the contrary, it is still a widely held belief that bright or gifted students require educational services above and beyond what is found in a mixed-ability, regular education classroom. Actually, research continues to show that in fact ability grouping can often be a smoke screen for segregation and damages students' self-esteem and school success. Ability grouping does not increase learning.

CLASSROOMS MAY RESULT IN A POWER STRUGGLE

Another reason to consider some supplemental, alternative strategies is that lectures can sometimes be a struggle-for-control battlefield.

The typical lecture format in a high school classroom supposedly looks like this:

> The teacher is standing at the front of the room while the students are sitting at desks or tables, organized in such a fashion that they have an easy view of the front of the room. They are expected to be silent and looking forward with a writing utensil in hand. The teacher lectures either alone or with the use of an overhead or electronic projector, chalkboard, or whiteboard. The students may have an outline from which to follow off or not, but they are usually expected to listen, glean important concepts, and record them on paper. Student-teacher dialogue is limited to teacher- or student-generated questions regarding the topic of the lecture.

In the movies and on television, this format looks great. The students are attentive and all engrossed in the topic of lecture. Humorous and pertinent questions and discussion are taking place in this active learning environment.

If I were to be truthful, I'd have to admit I have never had a class like that. Oh, I've come close on many occasions. In my advanced placement psychology and biology classes, the students are usually interested in a lecture and willing to take notes, and many times we do engage in fabulous dialogue. And in my general biology class, we have had terrific days of lecture, with dynamic student questions and discussion. Those are great days. I enjoy the class, and the students apparently do too.

However, to be honest, more than a few of my lecture days are not like that. People outside the realm of education may be shocked to learn that sometimes I've found students who would rather sleep than listen to my dynamic lecture on the biochemical pathway of the Krebs cycle. I must also admit that sometimes I have even had students who found the time better spent cleaning out their purse or backpack, writing a paper for their seventh period English class, doodling museum-quality pen and ink sketches of castles and knights, talking to the person next to them, discreetly playing games on their elaborate calculators, writing notes to pass between classes, or etching someone's name into the tabletop. And the list doesn't end there, but I'll stop for the sake of my ego.

This is not to say I'm not an interesting lecturer; really, I am. I can be funny, entertaining, and fascinating, right along with the next person. The problem is not with my lectures. The problem is not with the student. The problem simply is that the very best of teaching methodologies isn't always best for everyone, every day.

Preparing a lecture can be somewhat difficult but is usually enjoyable for a teacher who has an interest in the topic. Delivering the lecture to an interested and attentive group is relatively easy and again quite enjoyable for a teacher with an interest and a bit of a flair for delivering the information. But as we all know, delivering a well-prepared lecture to a group of 35 students when only seven or eight of them are either interested or able to learn and pay attention is grueling. It's more than that; it's exhausting, frustrating, disheartening, and self-defeating. The struggle for control in these classrooms can even lead many teachers to seek out early retirement. It doesn't have to be that way.

SOLUTION STRATEGIES

A good teacher does not have to forgo lecture. It can be—and perhaps, given your particular subject and population, should be—a significant part of your teaching strategy. But we can still allow for some alteration and supplemental activities to support our lecture in order to meet the needs of a wider population.

We all know many teachers who lecture extensively and have fabulous success with their classes. But we also realize that these teachers are usually the ones who teach things like honors chemistry, advanced placement American history, and calculus. They generally are not teaching the basic, everyone-has-to-take-this-to-graduate-high-school courses. That's an important distinction.

Courses that are successfully taught in a lecture-heavy format are usually courses that students *choose* to take. They are not required. Students choose to take an advanced math class, or an honors science class or a college course in English. The fact that students elect to take a class demonstrates two important factors in successful classrooms. First, the students must have some perception of self-choice, and second, students are generally most successful in those classes where the teaching methodology matches their learning style. Students in a lecture-heavy class are successful because they learn best or at least are capable of learning in a lecture format.

The great part to all of this is that we can add those same two factors to general classrooms as well. It is easy to add a choice component and easy to ensure that students are offered a learning strategy conducive to their learning style. When we do that, not only are the students more successful, but the teaching becomes a much more enjoyable experience as well.

I find that students in a general high school classroom fit into one of three basic categories when it comes to lecture-formatted classes. The first group (the attentive listeners) consists of a half dozen or so students who really enjoy listening to a lecture. They can easily attend to it and learn from it, and they prefer it to all other instructional strategies. These students will do well in high school and are sure to enjoy college, too. If you are lucky enough to get a room full of these, enjoy your lecture.

The second group (the fidgety listeners) are those who can tolerate a lecture, and their attention span may allow them to get bits and pieces of the content. They generally like to do something else while listening, such as doodling, coloring, or even cleaning out a backpack. They occasionally even ask a question. They may make up the bulk of the general classroom.

The third group (the nonlisteners) are those students who are lecture averse. They will not or cannot learn from this format and prefer to sleep through it, talk through it, or create disruptions. Teachers encounter our biggest power struggles with this group. While it is a small percentage of the classroom, it may create our biggest headaches.

The solution here is to offer choice and the perception of control to your students during the lecture time. It will increase the attention of the fidgety listeners and reduce the behavior problems found with the non-listeners. If you simply offer some alternate assignments or supplemental assignments that can be done during lecture, you can shift the perception of control around in your classroom.

Notice that I wrote *perception* of control. Offer your lectures as an option. Award points for them. Also offer assignments that students can do *during* the lecture while they listen and offer assignments students can do *instead* of the lecture.

So your lecture assignment may be offered something like this:

1. Listen to the lecture and take notes (with no other distractions). 25 points.

2. Quietly listen to the lecture while completing the gymnosperm life cycle diagram. Label parts and color. List five key ideas from the lecture on the back. 25 points.

3. Quietly complete the worksheet packet on gymnosperms. Form it into a booklet and make a full-color cover. 25 points.

The first assignment meets the needs of your attentive listeners. It is the traditional listen to the lecture and take notes assignment. You can use graphic organizers or preprinted outlines as note-taking aides, as you would in any traditional class.

The second assignment is what I call the "structured doodling" assignment as it allows students to do something with their hands while they listen. It is generally some type of art project that ties in with the lecture. Try to keep the art assignment simple so that it really is similar to doodling and does not get in the way of the lecture running in the background while they work. Maps, color projects, find-a-word puzzles, and book cover designs would all work as a structured doodling assignment.

The third assignment is for the hard-core nonauditory learner. Like it or not, they do exist—and for a variety of reasons. Some children have learning disabilities that truly prevent them from easily processing this type of information, some students cannot attend well to a lecture, and some just have very strong learning preferences in another arena.

You will find that the majority of students will actually choose the lectures and note taking. And the fact that they perceive it as of their own choosing will automatically increase their attention. Even those who choose to work on a completely different assignment (the nonauditory learners) can't help but overhear the lecture as they work, and the fact that you've empowered them with the perception of choice will significantly reduce your problem behaviors.

PERCEPTION IS EVERYTHING

Notice the difference here between reality and perception. The reality is that you, the teacher, are still maintaining the control and direction of learning in your classroom, but the students have the perception that they are in control of the situation. They, not the teacher, have made the decision as to what they are going to do today. Never underestimate the need of an individual to feel in control.

I cannot emphasize enough that the vast majority of behavior problems in classrooms are control issues. Shift the control, and the problems significantly decrease or disappear. Most of us in education know that students who are off task and disruptive are doing so for one of two reasons: either they are unable (or at least feel unable) to complete the task, or they are playing power games with the teacher in an attempt to maintain a sense of control. Both of these reasons are easy to eliminate.

GAIN CONTROL BY GIVING UP SOME OF IT

We can learn a lot about the psychology of perception from the advertising and media industry. Advertisers know a lot about perception and about shifting perception while never changing the reality. You can see this in action at your local car dealership.

A car dealership in my town recently offered a "zero percent interest or $2,00000 cash back" special on car purchases. This is a fairly common advertising ploy which most of us have seen before. It works very well and certainly helps sell cars. People think they are getting a terrific deal. People who choose the no-interest loan honestly believe they are getting a no-interest loan, and people who choose the cash really believe they are getting a cash rebate right into their pocket. Few people stop to realize that the perception is not the reality. In truth, the loan interest costs are built into the price, it's $2,000. If you prefer not to buy the car on a loan, the dealership will refund that up-front interest, which was added to the sticker price.

See how easy that works? If I want to sell you a $20,000 car, I just up the price to $22,000 and let you choose between a no-interest loan and a $2,000 cash rebate. I sell a lot more cars this way than I would if I advertised the car for $20,000 and offered to finance it for you for $2,000. I've simply changed the perception, not the reality.

The lesson here is an important one for teachers. Look at the difference in the emotions created in the two scenarios above. The first case is perceived by the consumer as a win-win situation and elicits positive emotions. The second case is perceived as a lose-lose situation and creates a neutral or negative emotional response. But the reality in both scenarios remains the same; only the perception has changed. By changing the perception, we've changed the emotional response.

You can do this in classrooms as well and change the whole dynamic by simply changing what emotions the students feel. Mrs. Eileen Sanders, a third grade teacher, has a strong belief in reading nightly at home. She is adamant that her students do this homework on a nightly basis. In fact, she has a policy of taking 15 minutes off the morning recess for any student who does not complete their homework reading requirement the night before.

Morning recess at Eileen Sanders's school lasts 30 minutes. Children who failed to do their homework the night before must stay in for the first 15 minutes as a punishment or a "consequence" for not doing their homework. Losing recess time for infractions is a rather common scenario in elementary classrooms. A visit to her class on any given day will show you a couple of dejected children waiting out their 15 minutes of lost recess time.

Mrs. Sanders can easily change the emotional response here by simply changing the perception of reality. Make morning recess 15 minutes long for everyone. All students who have completed their homework the night before get a 15-minute "bonus" added to their recess time.

Which classroom would you rather be in? Most of us would choose the second scenario because of the shift in the perception of control. The reality is the same—30 minutes of recess for those with completed homework, 15 for those without—but the perception has changed because of the way the information is presented to the students. The students in the second scenario now feel the situation under their control: a win-win situation and the positive emotions that go with it. "Anyone who finishes the homework gets a bonus" is always more pleasant than "anyone without their homework gets a punishment." Change the perception of control, and you've changed everything.

I find it advantageous to use this approach at every possible opportunity in my high school classroom. For example, I frequently grade exams on a curve. In other words, I grade everyone's test against the highest student score rather than a perfect score. It usually adds a few points to everyone's grade. In my first year of teaching, I had a problem when students who finished a test early would talk with others and disrupt the quiet for those still working. So I began a policy that those students who talked before everyone was done would not have their test scores curved. This created feelings of hostility and anger on the part of the students who perceived I was punishing them fairly or unfairly; it made no difference in their minds.

So, the next year I changed the policy and wrote it clearly on the board before every test:

> "Those students who can remain absolutely quiet until everyone has finished will have their exams graded on a curve, which will usually add a few points to the score."

No change in the reality, only the perception. But with that one simple change, the power of control was shifted from teacher to student, and the whole dynamic of the room changed.

Then it dawned on me that perhaps offering lectures blatantly as an option could do the same thing. Paying attention to the lecture was always an option anyway. Really, students can attend or not, and as we all know, some choose not to. So why not just change the locus of control: offer some alternatives to the lecture, and let go of it.

Of course, if you're going to offer the lecture as an option, you need to have other structured activities available that will also earn the student some class points and be a valid learning activity that will meet the same objective. What I found, though, was that when it is offered as an option, nearly everyone chooses the lecture. In the beginning several students try some of the other things, such as the structured "doodling" or the "no listening required" activity because they are novel, but eventually the majority of the students come back to the first assignment. Only now it is their choice, not mine, and those few hard-core, nonauditory learners still have a viable alternative to disrupting my lecture.

Rest assured that lectures can remain a significant part of the high school day. Again, differentiation asks us to make some simple additions to what we are doing, not subtract from what we are teaching. Many students benefit from lecture, and lectures can be one of the easiest and quickest ways to introduce a topic.

However, lecture time is also one of the most challenging parts of the class time in terms of behavior management. Despite the fact that we may be brilliant lecturers, there are always those students who don't share our enthusiasm for the topic or apparently prefer to learn in some other fashion.

PRACTICE ASSIGNMENTS FOR OVERCOMING THIS OBSTACLE

Practical Solution Idea 6.1: Award point values to your lectures and offer them as an option to other activities.

Practical Solution Idea 6.2: Design an alternate assignment that students can do instead of listening to the lecture. Make sure the assignment meets similar objectives.

Practical Solution Idea 6.3: Have some "structured doodling" types of assignments for students to work on during your lecture—posters, maps, illustrations, models, word finds, etc.

Q: Kathie, what do I do if I offer the lectures as an option and no one chooses them?

A: I can assure you, it won't happen. This is a common concern when teachers start thinking about empowering students to take responsibility for themselves. Sure in the beginning, students may choose something else, just because they can. They "play" with their new-found freedom. However, if you tie other assignments into the lecture, they soon discover that it is to their advantage to listen, and little by little they wander back. Funny thing, too, once they wander back, they actually are more attentive than ever because the task is now one of their own choosing. Even those who do choose one of the alternate assignments will undoubtedly "overhear" a bit of the lecture anyway. Just make sure that the students understand they must do something; doing nothing is not an option.

I Can't See How I Would Grade All Those Different Assignments

Chris Thomas has been teaching 11th grade algebra for 10 years. Students call her "hard." The line in front of her table at parent-teacher conferences is always longer than anyone else's. I've heard her say, "I just don't give A's first term."

Allen Hynes has been teaching ninth grade geology for 20 years. He's a brilliant man. Students call him "fun." His room is a museum. I've heard him say, "I tell the special ed department that they can send their kids to my room, and if they just sit and don't cause any disruptions, they can have a B."

Anne Lattrell has been teaching 10th grade biology for seven years. She's got a sweet disposition. Students call her "easy." Her room is called the island of misfit toys. While admiring a wonderful student-drawn poster in her room, I heard her say, "Oh, Enele did that. He just hardly ever came to class this term, and last week, before grades went out, he came to me in a panic because he had done nothing this term. He begged me to let him do a poster, and this is what he did. Isn't it great? After that I couldn't help but give him at least a passing grade."

A DESCRIPTION OF THE ISSUE

The issue of grading is a wide-gaping sore on the arm of education. In fact, it's so bad that we rarely dare discuss it. The injustices we see in the wide variety of grading schemes may make us angry, but we feel rather helpless to change the system.

This issue of grading and how to grade actually has two separate components. The first is how to logistically set up and manage a grade book or grading program when there are so many different assignments and not all students are doing the same ones. The second comprises the philosophical issues regarding how to award points and set standards in a classroom using differentiated instruction and assessment.

In both cases, the first thing we want to keep in mind is to keep it simple. You grade the success of the learning process, not the product. Your focus should be on the objectives learned, not necessarily the specific journey.

SOLUTION STRATEGIES

Setting Up a Paper or Electronic Grade Book

There are many ways to set up a grade book with differentiated instruction. You may want to play around with several in order to see which works best for you and your needs.

Entering Only Unit Grades and Exams

The way I've run my grade book for years is by simply entering unit grades. One unit, one grade. Each of my teaching units lasts for two weeks, and each is worth 100 points. I keep them to 100 points as it makes it easy to do percentages. Since my units are color coded, I enter them in the grade book by their color (each two-week Layered Curriculum student unit sheet is photocopied on paper of a different color). We complete four units in a grading quarter. Each quarter has a comprehensive quarter exam which is also worth 100 points, making the entire quarter worth 500 points. My grade book would look like this:

	Points					
Name	Red unit (100 possible)	Blue unit (100 possible)	Yellow unit (100 possible)	Pink unit (100 possible)	1st qtr exam (100 possible)	Total (500 possible)
Atherton, Jaime	88	76	90	98	88	
Andrews, Lonnie	76	73	67	82	74	
Barton, Sarah	78	71	73	65	78	
Boone, Drew	98	95	99	92	96	

This is a very simple system. The math is easy, and final grades are fairly simple to compute. The scores for individual assignments are marked directly on the student's Layered Curriculum unit sheet. After the unit score is entered in my grade book, I file all of those unit sheets away so that I can document and defend any grade to a parent, student, or administrator, if necessary.

Entering Grades by Subunits

Some teachers who use Layered Curriculum divide their grade books into the various layers to show a more detailed view of a student's performance.

						Points					
Name	*Red unit C* (30 pos.)	*Red unit B* (50 pos.)	*Red unit A* (20 pos.)	*Blue unit C* (30 pos.)	*Blue unit B* (50 pos.)	*Blue unit A* (20 pos.)	*Pink unit C* (30 pos.)	*Pink unit B* (50 pos.)	*Pink unit A* (20 pos.)	*1st qtr exam* (100 pos.)	*Total* (400 pos.)
Atherton, Jaime	30	40	18	28	45	19	30	45	20	88	
Andrews, Lonnie	25	38	10	29	43	8	28	40	17	74	
Barton, Sarah	27	43	19	28	48	17	30	49	20	94	
Boone, Drew	29	45	16	28	50	18	30	50	20	96	

This type of grading system works well if you need more detailed grades to post on your school Web site or if you need to issue weekly grades or periodic grades.

Entering Grades by Objectives

You can also set up your grade book based on the actual teaching objectives. This works well if you differentiate based on objectives. For example, you may offer your students a choice as to how they learn vocabulary or how they gather general information on a particular subject. The assignments would be given to students by objectives such as this:

Assignment 1. VOCABULARY for this unit (see whiteboard). Choose ONE. 10 points.

(a) Design picture-illustrated definition flash cards.

(b) Find two hard-print and three electronic source definitions for each term.

(c) Read glossary definition for each term and paraphrase it on paper. Share with a classmate.

Assignment 2. Listen to description of the New Deal. Choose TWO. 5 points each.

(a) Listen to teacher lecture Tuesday/Wednesday.

(b) Watch and listen to the video on the New Deal.

(c) In the listening center, listen to the text CD on Chapter 5, Section 2.

Assignment 3. Use a T chart to compare the New Deal to one of the following. Choose ONE. 10 points.

(a) JFK's New Frontier

(b) LBJ's Great Society

(c) Clinton's New Covenant

If you were setting up a grade book based on these objectives, then your grade program would reflect that, and grades would be entered as follows:

	Points			
Name	Unit 1 obj 1 (10 possible)	Unit 1 obj 2 (10 possible)	Unit 1 obj 3 (10 possible)	Unit quiz (20 possible)
Atherton, Jaime	8	10	8	18
Andrews, Lonnie	9	9	9	16
Barton, Sarah	8	5	9	20
Boone, Drew	10	9	9	18

Here each objective was given three assignment choices. So objective one, vocabulary, would be entered in column one, regardless of whether the student chose option a, b, or c. Again, we focus on the actual student learning rather than on the process each student chooses to meet the objective.

Daily or Weekly Grades

Another option for grading is to require or expect a certain number of points worth of work to be completed or mastered within a certain time period. For example, you may require one 10-point assignment to be completed each day, or 50 points worth of work to be completed each week. Your grade program or book then would reflect the daily or weekly total score. This works well if your school or district requires daily grades or a specific number of grades within a time period.

Design a Grade Scale by Considering "What's an A Worth?"

Now we come to the second component of grading, the thought process required to set value to student work, process, and learning.

What does a student need to do to earn a particular grade or mark in a class? This is one of education's big questions and a source of great debate. What is the meaning of a grade? How much should students be expected to know, demonstrate, or master in order to receive a particular mark or grade? How is it some high schools follow a 90–100 A, 80–89 B, 70–79 C, and so on, while others have a 93–100 A, 84–92 B, and so forth, and others leave the grades up to the individual teachers or departments? Some schools give letter grades, and some schools give number grades. If our school tells us that 93–100 is an A, what does a student need to do or learn to get a 93? Are the standards and expectations consistent across the department? Across the school?

We seldom give much thought as to where our traditional grading scheme came from or what the original thinking behind it was. Here again a little trek back in time may be in order. And in fact history tells us that from the very beginning of high school design, this issue of grading has left many feeling shaky. Let's visit with writer/educator Henry Morrison (1926), from the very early years of public high school, again.

> If we set up a given body of content to be absorbed, and fixed time limits within which the absorption process is to take place—and that is what the graded-school system necessarily implies—there can be but one outcome, human nature being what it is. Some pupils will do well, some indifferently, and some will not perform at all. Some will remember much, some little, and some none at all. But at the end of a year or a half-year, pupils must be moved onward to the next grade; or awarded some other kind of "credit."
>
> Shall we move only those who have remembered all? . . . Shall we move everybody? Clearly the absurdity would be too palpable. We must then move some and not others, and it will not do to retain so large a proportion that the process itself will come into disrepute. . . . If we send on a majority, in a land in which majorities have a peculiar sanctity, the public will believe that the elements of eternal verity are in the school. If we send on an overwhelming majority, the public will think we deal in "landslides," and landslide is the last word in political certitude. Eighty per cent is a safe majority here, 90 per cent there, and in some communities we dare not trust anything less than 97 or 98 per cent. . . . Seventy per cent is such a commonly-accepted passing grade, though any other would serve the purposes of our argument. . . . Nor can it be urged that 70 per cent stands for mastery and that higher grades stand for additional masteries.

And on what basis or criteria do we award points, marks, and grades?

> When the day of judgement arrives, we can draw the line at some convenient average percentile grade and in that way distinguish between the just and the intellectually unrepentant and wretched. Where shall the line be? Thus arises the passing grade as the learning objective. (pp. 42–43)
>
> The percentage does not represent a count; it is a symbol of the teacher's judgement of the value of performance when 100 per cent represents his valuation of a flawless performance. The average grade represents no quantity but simply the average of the numbers which stand as symbols of the teacher's judgement. (p. 47)

And so as this author so eloquently points out, grading is a very subjective term that varies according to teacher, community, and popular political standards. Probably at the very heart of the public's frustration with education is this arbitrary way of separating the successful from the unsuccessful in education.

Getting a passing grade has, unfortunately for many of our students, become the real goal of any high school course. And this is also the cause of what has come to be called the "get-by perversion": the idea that one needs to find out exactly which hoops one needs to jump through, what assignments need to be "done" and turned in, what basic information needs to be memorized for tomorrow's test so that one can get that very valued passing grade.

Two persistent problems have arisen with this system: (1) Students have missed the connection here between the process of doing an assignment and actual learning. (2) That passing grade has come to be a rite of passage, the actual line in the sand that determines whether one wears the uniform of a successful person or a failure.

Design a Grade Scale by Considering "What's an F Worth?"

Perhaps more important than what an A means is what an F means. I've failed; therefore I am a failure? I have not succeeded? I did not fulfill the expectation?

But were objectives explained, standards defined? In our system there may not necessarily be any expectation or predictability as to how many, if any, will even meet the objective.

At the beginning of a school year, each student sets out on a journey demarcated by an arbitrary set of points, objectives, and standards. Sometimes these are clear to students, but more often they are not. If you work hard, possess some talent, learn well using a linguistic-based model, persevere, and have a reasonable amount of aptitude, you pass, or at least you do not fail to pass.

But what if one or two of these ingredients is lacking, perhaps to a significant degree? Now you fail to pass. The term "failure" is quick to be attached by peers, parents, institutions, even yourself. But what does the F mean? Does it mean you did not work hard, or that you did not persevere, or that you lack reasonable aptitude, or that perhaps you don't process ideas well along linguistic lines?

It could mean any of these. Further, what great ideas, inventions, discoveries, and significant contributions to humankind have come without significant failure? Failure in general is not always a bad thing. There are many kinds of failure, and some should be encouraged. Think of original ideas and creative projects you yourself have done. Were they master-pieces on first attempt? Most likely no. In fact some of our greatest human contributions are the result of much failure.

Some failure should be encouraged and promoted in a learning situation. The notion that "failure is not an option" applies only to things like life-and-death situations and significant life events. If I'm going in for bypass surgery, I want absolute perfection. If I need a parachute while jumping from a plane, I don't want failure. Even if I take my car in to be repaired, I don't want failure. But I certainly expect there was a good deal of failure on the part of that surgeon, parachute designer, and mechanic in the process of preparing for their now successful endeavors.

Without failure, nothing changes. Mistakes, flaws, and brave ideas are the ingredients for discovery, art, and innovation. As von Oech (1990, p. 117) writes, "When everyone thinks alike, no one is doing much thinking."

In what ways can you promote the good kinds of failure? First by subdividing the term. After all, a person who tries and fails should always be lauded over the person who simply fails to even try. Encourage mistakes. Encourage and reward the creativity of the idea, the braveness in the effort, the fearless pursuit of an idea that challenges the status quo. Any student who makes a concerted effort for mastery and competence should be acknowledged for their perseverance and effort.

Otherwise we continue with what frequently occurs today: the student tries and stumbles, works harder, and becomes discouraged, then ends up with the letter grade of F for failure—the same grade given to the student who does absolutely nothing. It's easy to see how the learned helplessness that pervades so many of our high schools came to be. If we work very hard, but for some reason unknown to us, we fail, what use is it to ever try again? We are better off to just save our time and energy and ego.

PRACTICE ASSIGNMENTS FOR OVERCOMING THIS OBSTACLE

Reevaluate Grading Strategies

Practical Solution Idea 7.1: Replace F's or number scores that equate to F's with words of encouragement and acknowledgment of effort: "Almost,"

"Try Again," "Practice some more," "Let's meet about this topic," "Needs a little more work."

Reserve F or Fail grades for those who attempt nothing. F should be for "Failed to try." I met a teacher in South Carolina who has a grade schema like this:

93–100 A

84–92 B

75–83 C

1–74 NY

0 F

The NY means "not yet." Another teacher uses TA for "try again." It could also be SW for "still working." The point here is to acknowledge the effort and make all students aware that mastery, skill, and great ideas take work. If at first you don't succeed, try, try again.

Practical Solution Idea 7.2: Offer assignments where failure is required. In other words, students must show all attempts and reflections on each failure as they progress. In a math class, require the scratch paper or the prototypes for their model. In science require students to write about the errors made along the way and what they learned from them. In an English class, ask for more than one rough draft or revision. In any course, you may require students to take a quiz twice, showing the work they did to learn from their mistakes on the first one.

Self-reflection is important. A young genius engineer from the Massachusetts Institute of Technology was quoted on the Public Broadcasting System's *NOVA* as saying, "If you succeed on something without any failure, then you are just lucky, or . . . well, that's all really—you're just lucky. There is always failure to any great work."

Practical Solution Idea 7.3: Use collaborative groups to share failures and brainstorm solution strategies.

Encourage your students to seek out collegial support as they work toward mastery. Let them learn the advantages of teamwork and brainstorming. So often in adult life we get an idea, work on it, share our process with colleagues to help ourselves think through the revisions, and then work some more. Let students use that same process. There is a time for both individual work and teamwork.

I Thought Differentiated Instruction Was for Elementary Schools

I write this as I sit on a plane going from Chicago to Detroit. There are 119 other people on this plane. We are all going from Chicago to Detroit. The gentleman on my left is reading today's newspaper. I am working on this book. The man across the aisle is snoring in his reclined seat. The gentleman next to him is punching things into his palm digital organizer. Behind me is a young woman listening to her personal CD player while her mother types on a laptop computer.

We are all going from Chicago to Detroit. We all started in Chicago, are riding in the same plane, and will disembark in Detroit, but we all make the journey in our own style—a most adult thing to do. There are guidelines, of course, rules about when we can get up, when the electronic devices need to be turned off. Occasionally our work is interrupted by announcements, but in the end, we all arrive in Detroit.

Differentiation: allowing individuals to travel together to the same destination but with their own styles and by accommodating individual needs whenever possible. Sometimes you can't stand up. Sometimes you must power down your computer. Sometimes the crew needs everyone's attention up front. The restrictions are tolerated easily because we know that we are given freedom, when possible, to get our individual needs met.

What if the airlines did not subscribe to differentiation? What if it was all attendant directed?

"I need everyone to now get out their computers and power them up."

"But I didn't bring a computer," says 14B.

"Share with someone who came prepared" is the reply.

"I have no need to work on a computer. I want to listen to my music," chimes 22D.

"Well, we're not having music time right now. It's computer time."

"I need to use the restroom," shouts 11A.

"If you have a restroom pass, you can use it after computer time. 36A! Are you sleeping? Wake up! We're not sleeping our way to Detroit."

"But I'm tired," moans 36A.

"Well, I guess you should have gone to bed earlier last night."

"May I read the book I brought with me now as I'm not interested in computer work?" asks the one in 17C.

"Absolutely not. You can read your book on the next leg, from Detroit to Memphis. Right now we're doing our computers. If I have any more interruptions, we'll be staying on board for an extra five minutes after we get to the gate."

Sounds funny, doesn't it? That's because we are imagining a scene in which the characters are adults. No one would treat adults that way. We would never stand for it. Yet if we change the words slightly, we'll find the same scene in a chemistry class in Massachusetts.

"We're going to memorize the gases on the periodic table," announces the teacher.

"The what?" asks Joan.

"That's easy. We did this in junior high," shouts Martin.

"What's a period table?" asks Joan.

"Not period table, PERIODIC table," laughs Martin.

"Shhhh!"

"I'll explain later; just look in the back of your book."

"I have my own laminated table here in my binder," announces Bart.

"I hate this class already," grumbles Ian. "Wake me when it's over."

"Martin, you're not following along," reprimands the teacher.

"But I know all this already."

"Well, it will be a nice review then. . . . Ian, get your head off the table!" comes the teacher again as she tries to get everyone heading in the right direction.

"Oh my gosh! Do we have to memorize all this!?" exclaims Joan as she finds the periodic table.

"Can I use the hall pass?" shouts Ian.

"Not now. We're in the middle of something," laments the teacher.

"The middle of what?" asks Ian.

"We're looking at the periodic table!" comes the frustrated response from the teacher.

"Oh, well, I brought the wrong book, so can I use the hall pass anyway?"

Ever had one of these days? Me too.

This class may have run a bit easier if there were a couple of assignment choices, a lecture offered to those who needed to learn or review gases, and an alternative tactile activity, such as a computer program on gases (for the Ians in the room).

A DESCRIPTION OF THE ISSUE

Perhaps the separation between elementary and secondary teaching is a relatively simple matter called diffusion of responsibility.

If you teach third grade, you have one set of kids all day long. You are their sole teacher or at least have them for the lion's share of the day. If a child isn't doing well in your class, you must assume nearly all the responsibility. But if you teach 10th grade, you are but one of six or eight teachers each child has. You can share the blame. If you add in guidance counselors, assistant principals, and other support people in the building, you can really cut your share of the responsibility pie down to a very small piece.

In addition to the issue of diffusion of responsibility, there are practical differences between elementary and secondary teaching. The smaller student loads in elementary school allow the teachers to do extensive research on the educational history of their students. Elementary teachers can track a student's progress, talk with last year's teacher, and see how things have been developing educationally for a student.

It is much easier too for the elementary teacher to be aware of the various strengths and weaknesses of a particular student across disciplines. You know that Heather struggles with science yet blooms in history because you have Heather for both science and history.

But a high school teacher with a 150 to 220 student load rarely has time to pull and study extensive school records. Nor do we generally have time to talk to all of a student's other teachers to discover the student's individual strengths and weakness. We may mistakenly think that a child's performance in our class is representative of how the child performs across the board, never realizing that the student has significant strengths or weaknesses in other subjects.

It is easier sometimes for elementary teachers to tailor assignments for a student because they are privy to this information. If I know that Henrie really enjoys art and has tremendous confidence and feelings of self-efficacy in this area, then I know to try to incorporate art choice into some subjects that are more difficult for him. The secondary teacher, however, has to hope to stumble upon such insights. It takes at best several weeks to get to know your students enough to discover and learn their interests and learning strengths.

Perhaps the biggest difference between elementary and secondary school is found in the philosophy of differentiated instruction through student centered classrooms. Traditional student centered models have been relegated to elementary classrooms. When most of us picture a student centered room, we picture students in centers. The mental model of centers with alphabet blocks just doesn't fit with our taller, more developed teenage students.

Classic student centered approaches such as Montessori tend to run at best through about the sixth grade. Most resources for student centered models are geared for elementary teachers, and articles showing active, engaged learners tend to feature photos of youngsters working in art centers or sitting on carpet squares on the floor. Rarely does a high school teacher see visual representations of 16-, 17-, and 18-year-old students working in learning centers, stations, or active classrooms. About the closest thing we see to that image is a science fair.

SOLUTION STRATEGIES

The truth, however, is that differentiation works beautifully at the high school level. Children are children; some are just taller than others. And children have a natural curiosity about the world. They like to learn. They like to discover and play with things and ideas and concepts. Just because children are 15 or 17 years old does not mean they don't like to explore new areas.

Differentiated classrooms take advantage of the child's natural curiosity. And a differentiated high school classroom has the advantage of having much more capable learners who can apply their discoveries in a much more complex manner.

Find what your students enjoy naturally and try to incorporate your subject into their natural world.

PRACTICE ASSIGNMENTS FOR OVERCOMING THIS OBSTACLE

Don't be afraid to borrow some ideas from our peers in elementary education. Take many of the ideas that come from elementary schools and spin them to fit your population. Traditionally, elementary schools do keep a rather student centered approach to learning. The same principles and ideas that work with younger children can be applied to more difficult subjects. And of course best of all, our students are intellectually more mature. Unlike elementary students, our students can think more abstractly and more globally and are more idealistic about the world. They have more personal background, and their brains are at a very different stage of development.

Practical Solution Idea 8.1: Divide your room into resource centers.

Put printed, bound material, such as textbooks, library books, and reference materials, in one location. Put art materials in another section. Divide off one corner as a video-watching area (use headphones for the sound). Allow students to move around to gather material from the centers or actually provide workspace in these areas.

Practical Solution Idea 8.2: Allow a wide range of developmentally appropriate materials.

Remember that not all your students are strong readers. Make sure you have text and reference materials to allow all your students the opportunity to gather information in printed form. Some students think and reason better with materials they can manipulate. Some students do better when they can talk through their problem-solving strategies. Allow space and opportunity for students to work in a variety of settings with a variety of materials.

Practical Solution Idea 8.3: Assign jobs.

Have different students monitor areas or complete class tasks. Don't be afraid to use some of the large wall hanging models that match students to jobs which are frequently found in first grade classrooms. Jobs could include things like textbook monitor, art supply lender, lab maintenance monitor, or video center monitor.

Practical Solution Idea 8.4: Teach through art.

Probably the most obvious avenue into the adolescent world is their music. As I will elaborate on a little later in this book, due to the nature of art and the nature of the adolescent brain, art speaks the language of the adolescent. And of course their favorite art form is usually music.

Take advantage of this opportunity. Use youth music and other art forms to help students apply and understand new concepts. We see a lot of music and art used and taught in high school, but it is seldom their art, the art that speaks to today's youth. Classical art is wonderful, as are jazz and modern symphonic music, but that's not what most of our students use as the vehicle of emotional expression in their popular culture. As difficult as it may seem to you, look for ways to tie your teaching into today's youth art. Popular movies, music, and graffiti are expressions of their new emotional explorations—the centerpiece of adolescence. Can you find recurring themes of history in some of today's music or movies? Can you find math patterns? Can you tie in science principles to films or modern poetry? Can you find contemporary music to reflect contemporary world issues?

One of the things elementary educators do so very well is to take their cues from the students. They watch for natural developmental interests and tie into those. We as high school educators should be doing the same thing. Start taking some cues from your students.

I Subscribe to Ability Grouping

As every parent and educator knows, students come in a wide variety and never fail to surprise us with their unique personalities and behaviors. One year I even had a student bring a head for show-and-tell. We didn't really have structured show-and-tell in 10th grade, but you know how kids bring things in that they think fit the instructional topic. Anyway, the young man brought a head. A real one. It was a real human head. He said his dog had brought it home a few months ago and his family thought it was "cool," so it now resided on the family's coffee table. No one prepares you for days like this in the classroom. There is nothing in any education or teaching book or course I took that covered the topic of human heads for show-and-tell. Yes, we handled it. It's a long story involving the Federal Bureau of Investigation, a very irate mother, and a wonderful student resource officer who had a lot of diplomacy. It will certainly remain one of my more memorable teaching days.

That same year, I had a student playing around with the plastic model of a human skull I had in my classroom. You have probably seen these models as they are quite common in a biology classroom. The top lifts off to show a plastic brain housed within. One of my students lifted the top and asked what that thing inside was.

"Why, that's the brain" was my reply.

"For reals, Ms. Nunley! That's where your brain is? Wow!" He was awestruck.

The student was 17 years old and had just discovered that your brain is located inside your head.

A DESCRIPTION OF THE ISSUE

In my years of high school teaching, I have had students who really challenged me because they were so intelligent and quick that I struggled to come up with things to stretch their minds. I have had students with charm and personality so grand that you nearly forgave them for anything. I have had students who worked so slowly they stretched my patience to its limits and students who were so full of energy they sometimes made me reconsider my decision to be a teacher.

Students' instructional plans need to be different because our students are so very different. But this individual instruction idea gets hung up in our traditional view of fairness. Is it fair to give one student the same grade as another student when the first student was doing a different amount or type of work?

Most of us know that traditional IEP modifications assigned to individual special education students have created grading nightmares for teachers. Elaborate grading practices have been developed to handle these special situations, and these practices have exacerbated the old argument about fairness.

Perhaps educators have confused the meaning of fairness with the term "equal" or "same." But fair doesn't mean everyone is treated the same. In fact, people frequently need to be treated differently in order for circumstances to be fair. If two siblings are sick, does anyone complain about fairness if the treatments are different? What if one child gets better quicker than the other. Do their treatments need to remain the same so as to be fair?

If two students are in math class, and one of them has already mastered his times tables and the other one still struggles a great deal with times tables, should they both have to practice and do the exact same assignment for things to be fair? Most of us can see that it may be absurd to treat everyone the same all the time. People are different, so their prescriptions for learning must be different.

Lecture-heavy classrooms frequently promote ability grouping and segregate many populations of special needs students. Although it is still widely believed that bright or gifted students require educational services not found in the regular classrooms and although the vast majority of high school teachers think students learn best when grouped by ability, ability grouping is often a smokescreen for segregation and does little to improve our students' feeling of self-efficacy and self-esteem (Manning & Lucking, 1990; Stainback & Stainback, 1992; Weaver, 1990; Renzulli, Reis, & Smith, 1993; Willis, 1995).

Certainly many teachers find it easier to teach to a group of students with little variation in ability level. This is especially true in classrooms that are primarily dependent on the lecture-textbook method.

SEGREGATION WITHIN THE CLASSROOM

One of the misconceptions found among teachers differentiating instruction is the belief that lower-functioning children needn't waste time on higher-thinking skill assignments. We may be tempted to believe that the basic skills are good enough for our lowest-ability students—or that perhaps they are in our room primarily for "social skills" and to learn a few basic concepts.

Teachers may feel that their time is best spent on the most gifted and talented students and that in fact extra effort should be spent challenging our brightest learners. Furthermore, complex application and critical thinking assignments and skills may be reserved for those most intellectually competent individuals.

The danger in this type of thinking is that it is based on the idea that only our most gifted students will be called on to be the decision makers in our society. A quick look around the real world will show the fallacy of this thinking.

Do we see only gifted and talented people become leaders? Look at the people who currently run our countries, our states, and our cities. Look at corporate executives, school board members, city council members, legislators, small-business owners, decision makers, voters, and parents. Did they all come from the pool of gifted students?

Look around your classroom. Consider each student. Think of the most gifted, the least gifted, the most dysfunctional, your personal favorite, the one who frightens you, the one who makes you laugh, the one from the most unstable family background, the one most intellectually challenged. Do you know what all these students have in common?

When they turn 18, every one of those children will be eligible to vote. All of them. And like it or not, their vote will count as much as yours. Every one of the kids in our school will one day be a contributing member of our society. They will be voting on such things as who will lead our country, our state, and our city. They will vote on regulations for the nursing homes we may one day be living in. They will vote on issues such as genetic engineering, stem cell research, war, health care, education, and environmental issues. They will be leaders of people. They may lead nations, companies, and school boards. They will raise children.

Do you think only the very gifted students become leaders? Voters? Parents? We must prepare every child in our room to be a complex, critical thinker because that's what adulthood asks of people. And it asks it of all adults, not just the gifted or even the above average. Our society asks complex, critical thinking of all the people—even those we term "below average."

Where do all these people learn critical thinking skills? I should hope they are learning them in our schools. But if we continue to track students at an early age so that only the brightest and traditionally gifted students get to learn how to think critically and make the big decisions, what will that mean to our future? That type of thinking works in a society that lets only the brightest vote, lead, and decide things for the rest of the people. We do not live in that society. We live in a system that is run by all the people, so shouldn't our schools reflect that thinking as well?

PREPARING GLOBAL THINKERS

Regardless of the community positions our students take as adults, one thing is for certain: There will be a greater need for all workers to be global participants. Differentiated instruction encourages all students to think more complexly, problem solve, and develop a greater tolerance and understanding of the diversity among people.

John Kotter (1988), of the Harvard Business School, writes frequently about the increased need for leaders in today's dynamic world. He says the deregulation of industry and the new global economy have changed the role of managers and business people. Businesses, communities, and governments need people with keen leadership skills. Our schools must actively plan for the teaching of these skills.

Since the business world first started focusing on this issue in the early 1980s, it has become even more important. We see globalization today on a scale no one would have even imagined just 25 years ago. The last two decades in particular have witnessed an astonishing development of global industries. Tomorrow's leaders need to be sensitive to diversity and various cultural perspectives.

Globalization, technological changes, global competition and rivalry, workforce diversity, and the new customer expectations of better, faster, cheaper have brought major changes to the way businesses operate. The focus in business today is teams, team building, team diversity, and global sensitivity.

There is no better way to teach these skills than in a mixed-ability classroom that offers different instructional strategies and team collaboration opportunities and where all children are encouraged to think about complex issues. Extensive research supports the use of complex, critical thinking activities with all levels of learners (Raudenbush et al., 1993; King & Kitchener, 1994; Lambert & McCombs, 1998; Zohar et al., 2001; Zohar & Dori, 2003; Torff, 2003, 2005; Dolezal et al., 2003).

SOLUTION STRATEGIES

Keep a wide variety of assignments that give students multiple options for ways to gain basic knowledge. Make sure you have simple tasks offered that your lowest-ability student can complete and very complex assignments that stretch your highest-ability student. Make the more complex assignments worth more points so that they appeal to your higher-ability student. Your lower-functioning student may have to do several of the smaller point assignments to equal the points another student earned from completing just one tougher assignment, and that's okay. This is a critical point for educators.

It is okay if you have some students working harder and doing more assignments than others.

Is it fair? Life's not fair. I learned that from my mother, who said to me many times, "Kathie, life is not fair. Never has been, never will be."

Is it fair that my son with dyslexia has to take one hour to read what a classmate reads in 10 minutes? No, but that's life. Is it fair that I have to spend hours working, weeding, and praying over my paltry three-foot flower garden when my neighbor can apparently whip up a blue-ribbon arboretum in her yard overnight? No, but that's life. She's got a gift for gardening whereas I apparently am gardening disabled (we'll call it GD for the sake of education, where everyone gets an alphabet label).

I have actually seen classrooms where teachers are told to give students with certain disabilities "bonus points." For example, add 15 points to the assignment for a student who is learning disabled. My first question is "Do you remove 15 points from the assignments of gifted students?" For to be fair, if that is your policy for learning disabled students, then it should be for the gifted and talented too.

Let me reiterate my earlier bold statement of an idea that should have been understood and accepted long ago: *It's okay if special ed kids have to work harder or longer on some things.*

Did I really say that?

Yes. And let me clarify my point. Students with special needs do not need things easy—just reasonable. And that means they probably are going to have to work harder and longer on many activities than their classmates who may not share those same disabilities. In fact, a classroom where special ed kids are not working at all or hardly at all should be a cause for real concern.

There is a common misconception in many schools that students from the special ed population need to be excused from learning. There's a belief that somehow these kids don't need to learn the same things as other students or that they need a very easy road. I think we have lost sight of education for all.

If an IEP modification says "spelling doesn't count for this child," that is not the same thing as "spelling doesn't matter" or "spelling is not important." Spelling does matter and spelling is important. In the real world, spelling is important. People make all kinds of judgments and assumptions based on a person's ability to write, and spelling influences those judgments. So "spelling doesn't count" may mean that a teacher is not allowed to count off points for spelling. However the child should still be expected to work on and improve his or her spelling.

As an adult, if I can't spell because of some significant learning disability, I had better learn some pretty effective ways to compensate for that or it will have an effect on my life. I had better learn to use a spell-checker and a grammar-checker or hire a proofreader or a good secretary or bribe my roommate with chocolate chip cookies to proofread, or find some other solution strategy. What is not an option is to have sticky notes attached to all my resumes, letters, documents, and business correspondence that say "Spelling doesn't count."

So what do you say to the student who truly struggles with spelling and whose IEP states that you are not to "count" it? I'd say, "We won't dock you points for misspelled words, but what kind of strategies can we come up with so that you can get most of your work turned in with very few spelling and grammatical errors?"

What about a student who needs extended time on assignments or a reduction in class work? A strategy here may be to subdivide all your assignments and divide the points up accordingly. Offer all students the option of doing bits and pieces.

Allow not just students with IEPs but any of your students working to the best of their ability to ask for extended time for extenuating circumstances. Have the student make a reasonable time frame for when they can get assignments completed. Make all your students understand that you are willing to work with them on their individual issues and struggles but that having a disability is not an excuse from working hard and learning. We all have disabilities. The secret to success in life is finding ways to compensate for them so you can get the job done, one way or another.

Life will not be easy for persons with disabilities. Like it or not, it just won't. We are not doing these students any favors by trying to make things easy for them. What we need to do is help them see how they too can reach their absolute best potential and how to compensate in the world for their weaknesses by capitalizing on their strengths.

You may not be able to write, but you are an excellent typist. You may not be able to comprehend well what you read, but you are an excellent listener. You may not be able to put your complex ideas in a written form, but you are an excellent artist with an ability to communicate in graphic forms.

PRACTICE ASSIGNMENTS FOR OVERCOMING THIS OBSTACLE

Rather than trying to make things easy for students with disabilities, we should be helping them learn to compensate. And we should be removing as many obstacles to their learning as we can, just as we would for our regular education students. We must help all our students discover their strengths and allow them to learn through these strengths.

Practical Solution Idea 9.1: Offer whole-class modifications.

If you've been asked to make some type of modification to your instruction for one particular student, make that modification available to all. We'll elaborate on this idea later in this book (see Chapter 12), but make sure you provide enough variation so that all your learners can succeed. Maintain high expectations for all students. Try NOT to make accommodations available only to a select group.

Practical Solution Idea 9.2: Take advantage of the Pygmalion effect.

Expect a lot from your students and they will give you a lot. The field of psychology offers us an insight known as the Pygmalion effect (Rosenthal & Jacobson, 1992). One of the leading authorities on the subject, Robert Rosenthal, teamed up with school principal Lenore Jacobson nearly 40 years ago to show how this so-called self-fulfilling prophecy can work in public school classrooms. While the original study was conducted in elementary classrooms, the results have been replicated in more than 500 different studies in high schools, colleges, and business settings since. In what is now a classic study, Rosenthal discovered that teachers' expectations can in fact affect students' intellectual performance. In other words, the IQ scores of students can actually go up simply because their teacher expects them to. (See Sidebar)

In 1968 Harvard researcher Robert Rosenthal teamed up with school principal Lenore Jacobson in South Dakota. They tested all the students in Jacobson's school with a general IQ test, which they pretended would measure "academic blooming," a predictor of students who were going to grow intellectually in the coming school year. After the test, they chose about 20 percent of the student body by means of a random number generator and issued false reports to those students' teachers. They told the teachers that these select students in their room had scores that indicated they would really grow intellectually in the coming school year. Remember, these students were selected completely at random.

At the end of the year, Rosenthal and Jacobson retested all the students in the school. On average, all the students in the school gained about 12 IQ points over the course of the year, except for the special, randomly chosen group that had been reported to their teachers as promising to show extraordinary intellectual gains. This group gained an average of 27 IQ points! So students do get smarter when expected to get smarter by their teachers.

(Continued)

(Continued)

> The researchers did several classroom visits throughout the year and observed things teachers do with and for students for whom they have favorable expectations. They broke their observations down into what they called the "four key factors":
>
> - Warmth
> - Climate
> - Response opportunity
> - Input
>
> Simply put, if teachers have high expectations for students, they are nicer to them, provide a better climate for learning, allow more time for them to respond, and help them work through their answers to elaborate their thinking and simply teach more material to them.
>
> Rosenthal himself is quick to note that it is very difficult to know exactly what to do with the information this research provides, but it is most definitely food for thought for any educator (Rosenthal, 1991).
>
> So, look for the good in your students and you will find it.

I Have Real Logistic Issues

A DESCRIPTION OF THE ISSUE

Many of us are excited about student centered and differentiated instruction. We have the vision, we've been to the inservices, and we have designed some lessons. Then the logistic issues stop us dead in our tracks. Physical limitations in our room, a lack of a dedicated classroom, liability concerns, and population size can all create obstacles for even the most enthusiastic differentiated instructor. Let's go back to our opening philosophy: the larger the problem, the more creative the solution. Even some very daunting logistic issues can be overcome with some modification.

SOLUTION STRATEGIES AND PRACTICE ASSIGNMENTS FOR OVERCOMING THESE OBSTACLES

Liability Issues

Safety can be a major concern in student centered classes. Most of us agree that teacher centered classrooms are safer when laboratory or other adult or dangerous equipment is involved. We can see the problems that arise if a group of students is simply allowed to play with the Bunsen burner in one corner, while the teacher is lecturing in another corner, and another group of students is mixing chemicals in an attempt to melt the rubber off the table legs in another corner. Liability issues are a genuine concern when differentiating instruction, but they are solvable issues.

Practical Solution Idea 10.1: When safety is an issue, try to isolate activities to particular class days or time periods.

Use these high-risk activities with a whole-class instruction approach. For example, if you are teaching a chemistry class, have particular days allocated to labs. Limit the variation in the labs, and keep dangerous-equipment stations in one location so that you can monitor them. Labs involving chemicals, fires, electricity, sharp objects, and other potential dangers would be located at physically close areas, and you would be stationed there for the vast majority of the class time. If you want to offer some variety, you can do that within the same lab station setting or offer safer, alternative assignments in another area.

Practical Solution Idea 10.2: Buddy up with another teacher and allow the students to move between the rooms.

In this strategy, one teacher would always be monitoring the lab or shop, and the other teacher would be monitoring the other activities or lecture/seatwork. This works particularly well if you share a lab or shop area. If the lab is open every day to all students, it makes it easier on both teachers and students.

> Andrew Kimmer and Barbara DeChambeau share a life science lab between their two rooms. Previously they scheduled alternate days for the labs. Now they work units together, and on Mondays both teachers offer in-class work only. Then starting on Tuesday, Mr. Kimmer stays in the lab and Ms. DeChambeau works in her room. Students who are ready to begin the lab head in there to work. Students needing more time for nonlab work go to Ms. DeChambeau's room. On Wednesday, Thursday, and Friday, they swap roles back and forth between lab and class. If one room becomes overpopulated, they ask some students to move back into the other room. They love the teaming. The two teachers have had to make a few adjustments, such as the way they handle their consultation or off periods, as those periods don't match. (They donate one off period each week to work in the lab and do their planning while supervising the labs.) They find the benefits outweigh the adjustment issues as the team concept has so many advantages for both them and their students.

Scheduling Issues

Related to the liability issue are scheduling problems. How do you differentiate if your entire class has to go to the computer lab all together? What happens if you have access to the video player only on certain days? What if your media specialist allows students only when accompanied by a teacher? What if you are renting a video or DVD and you only want to rent it for one day? What if you are having a substitute on Thursday? The list of issues is nearly limitless.

Q: Kathie, how do you control materials so that you don't lose them? Lab equipment, dissection kits, even colored pencils tend to disappear.

A: I solved most of these problems by implementing an "issue system" in my room. I used plastic cigar boxes or large pencil cases. Each box was numbered in permanent marker and had two 3×5 inch cards enclosed with the contents. The cards listed the exact contents of the box.

Art boxes contained a set of colored pencils, colored markers, glue stick, small scissors, and sticky notes. One student was art box librarian for the month. He or she issued them to students by keeping their signed 3×5 card upon issue. This librarian was responsible for checking kits for completion when returned.

I used a similar system for dissection kits, CDs, videos, and headphones.

Practical Solution Idea 10.3: Don't hesitate to use whole-class instruction for some activities.

Here again, we use the solution for liability protection in that we may need to isolate some student activities to a particular day. If you have access to a video only on a certain day, require that activity to be done then. You can still differentiate the day if you want, but that particular activity can be done only that day. So tell the students, "The video option is only available this Wednesday. If you are doing that activity, plan to do it Wednesday." Or you may let them know that on Tuesday and Thursday of this week, you will be meeting in the media center. If they need to use the media center, those are the days to do it. If they don't need the media center, they should make sure they bring some materials with them in order to work on some activity that can be completed there in the media center.

Practical Solution Idea 10.4: Try to have technology integrated within the school rather than isolated.

We still find computer labs commonplace in schools. A high school may have two or three dedicated rooms filled with computers and Internet access. If you want to use the room, you need to schedule it ahead of time. This is extremely limiting to the differentiated classroom.

Work very hard at your site to have those labs moved and dispersed throughout the building so students can integrate technology and technological resources in their everyday learning. Having two or three computers in each room is a much better use of this equipment. Now you can offer computer assignments as options, and your students can use the resources available for all their activities.

The Room Is Too Small

As I mentioned earlier, many teachers have a mental model of student centered classrooms looking like a kindergarten class of learning centers and stations. This model requires a great deal of space. Student movement in cramped quarters seems dangerous.

You don't necessarily need a lot of space. So don't let the physical limitations of the room and desks get in the way of planning instructional variation. Differentiated instruction can be successful in any type of classroom and any size. I remember the year I had 51 students in a general biology classroom that could seat 38! The good news was that it forced me to be creative in seating and workspace. If you have a small space or just too many students for the space you have, then movement will be somewhat limited and controlled for purely survival reasons.

Practical Solution Idea 10.5: Limit student movement if necessary.

While you may envision the ideal differentiated classroom as resembling San Francisco's Exploratorium, most of us don't have the luxury of that kind of space. While students may wish for the freedom to move from task to task whenever the whim strikes, the logistics of the room may not allow it. Structure student movement so that it is limited to certain times. Put materials in specific places in the room, but limit access time.

When I have had extremely large classes, I allowed five minutes of "move time," when students could get up, get their materials, and then get to their work spot for the rest of the class period. If they were heading to the library, this was the time to get their library pass. If they were going to watch a video, this was the time to claim their spot and headphones in the video corner. If they were getting texts or lab materials, they would get them or check them out and get to their work spot.

We utilized floor space and windowsills as work areas. Even in my smaller classes, we found that moving desks around a bit to allow floor space was a nice option, especially late in the day, when some of my taller students had had just about all the "seat time" they could handle.

Keep materials in centers and let the students go get the materials and then go back and work in their traditional workspace or desk. A hanging file folder makes a great system for a variety of worksheets or handouts. You can number the hanging folders to correspond with the number of the assignment on the students' assignment menu sheet. So if assignment 7 is a map to label, then hanging folder 7 contains those maps.

Practical Solution Idea 10.6: Try different classroom designs.

Play around with different seating and grouping arrangements. Don't be afraid to remove some of the desks. You obviously cannot move the four walls or add windows, but you can artificially change the shape of a room with furniture and desk grouping (Dyck, 1994; Meek, 1995).

The "Fat L"–shaped classroom is one that many new schools are utilizing as it gives so many options for teacher-dependent and teacher-independent grouping. While most of us have the plain rectangular shape, we can create an artificial Fat L by blocking off one corner of the room with a teacher area or quiet-reading corner (see Figure 10.1).

Try different desk and table arrangements. We're all familiar with the rows all facing forward. That works great if you use a lot of teacher-directed, whole-class instruction.

But seating everyone is a giant square with the teacher at any one of the desks within the square works well for facilitating group discussion.

Figure 10.1   Fat L classroom and Pseudo-Fat L classroom

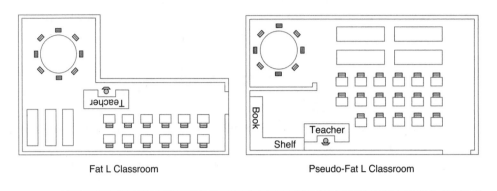

Fat L Classroom   Pseudo-Fat L Classroom

A horseshoe shape with the teacher near the mouth of the horseshoe also works well for group discussion.

But for student work time, look for different groups of seats and a variety of work surfaces.

You want to create some settings that encourage group work. Group projects and cooperative learning groups emphasize and encourage learning as a team. This type of learning fosters cooperation and sharing of ideas that will enable students to process material better. While learning alone can occasionally have some benefit, grouping is usually a preferred method of learning. That was the point of all our study groups in college. Rather than struggle along as an individual, we could get together and use the strengths of the group to decrease the time it took to learn something. And grouping actually increases the amount of information absorbed. Add some large tables with chairs. Floor space with carpet squares works too. Lab tables can be arranged in a variety of ways to encourage small-, medium-, and large-group work.

Make sure your teaching style matches the classroom design. Don't put all your student desks in four square cooperative groups if you lecture most of the time. This just gives a sizable number of students a kink in their neck from craning around. If you move back and forth between lecture and independent work, try individual student clipboards, and let the students move their chairs around just for the lecture. Cutting large sheets of shower board, which you can get at any home improvements store, into lap-size pieces can produce inexpensive lap desks. These are great for making inexpensive personal whiteboards too.

Practical Solution Idea 10.7: Free up space for student work areas.

If you're really short on space, share instructional areas, resources, and storage with a colleague. Can you find a central place for book storage, lab equipment, or video supplies? Buddy up and share labs, instructional materials, reading areas, and so forth. Try a "reading zone" in each department. These are absolute-quiet areas for students to read but are shared by more than one teacher. I know teachers who team up and take turns having the absolute-quiet classroom. When students are doing an assignment that requires absolute quiet, they use classroom A, and when they are doing assignments that require some classmate interaction or where some noise can be tolerated, they use classroom B.

If your classroom adjoins another one, try some variation of that buddy system mentioned earlier. Take turns supervising and assisting different tasks. Even if you don't share the same discipline, you may find a day or two a week when you can cooperate on room use.

Practical Solution Idea 10.8: Think outside your walls!

We get so self-contained that it blocks our creative process. Can you use some of the hallway outside your door? Is there a way to share storage space or study space? If teachers work in their empty rooms during their consultation or off period, would they mind once a week allowing a student or two to work in their absolute-quiet classroom? Can students needing a quiet study carrel utilize the In School Suspension room? Discuss some of these ideas as a faculty and see what you can come up with. Try to break away from the traditional limitations of one set of students belonging to one teacher in one classroom all doing the same thing.

I Want My Classroom Under Control

A DESCRIPTION OF THE ISSUE

One of the main reasons many teachers resist differentiated approaches to teaching is they think it will cause them to lose control in their classrooms. Teachers like control. They like to have classes that are in control and often have a genuine fear that to relinquish any control at all to the students would ultimately lead to chaos. I have actually been in some classrooms where the teachers spend so much time on control that it becomes their biggest source of pride. Whether or not learning is occurring is beside the point when what matters most is the control they have over their students.

People want some control. If you don't give it to them, they will find ways to take it. The perception of lack of control causes chronic stress, slows the learning process, can make one physically ill, and causes classroom management problems (Kern et al., 2001; Adelson, R., 2004; Duman et al., 1999; Pine et al., 1999; McEwen & Magarinos, 2001; Olff, 1999; Deci, 1995; Wyers, Dohm, & Ayers, 2001).

One of the leading researchers in the field of control and its effect on the classroom is Edward Deci. Deci and his team have been carrying out research in this field since the early 1980s. His findings: The more we control others, the more their behavior needs to be controlled.

> It is truly amazing, as pointed up by our findings that if people are ongoingly treated as if they were either passive mechanisms or barbarians needing to be controlled, they will begin to act more and more that way. As they are controlled, for example, they are likely to act more and more as if they need to be controlled. (1995, p. 84)

What all this research is showing is that allowing people to feel they are in control actually reduces classroom problem behavior. And autocratic, or control-oriented, classrooms actually encourage irresponsibility. If the teacher makes all the decisions and rules, then students have to assume no responsibility.

PERCEPTION OF CONTROL TRUMPS ALL

Never underestimate the importance of one's need for control. It is a basic need, and people will go to great lengths to get it, sometimes at a cost of even logic or reason. In fact we can sometimes put ourselves in real danger simply to ensure some perception of control. I saw a perfect example of this two years ago as I was driving through Michigan.

It was the Wednesday preceding Thanksgiving, and I was returning to the Detroit airport. The highways were filled with cars. What should have taken me an hour took nearly twice that long due to the bumper-to-bumper traffic. The radio announcer read off the traffic report and mentioned that this was expected to be one of the heaviest auto-travel Thanksgiving weekends in history. Apparently the fears from the September 11, 2001, terrorist attacks were lingering, and this was reflected in a new attitude that people would rather drive than fly to their Thanksgiving plans. Even drives of six or seven hours seemed preferable to people over facing their fears of air travel.

Here is the perfect example of the need for feeling in control overriding logic and reason. Logic tells us that the chance of anyone in the United States being killed in a commercial plane crash over the Thanksgiving holiday is extremely small. In fact there's a real strong likelihood that no one will die in a commercial plane crash over that weekend.

We also know that several hundred people will die in highway traffic accidents over the same weekend. Traffic deaths are fairly predictable, given the historical data (see Figure 11.1). Various automobile clubs even

Figure 11.1   Deaths due to vehicle accidents on roads and interstates and commercial air travel in the United States over the Thanksgiving weekend (Wednesday through Sunday)

Year	Traffic deaths on highways*	Commercial airline deaths**
2000	509	0
2001	585	0
2002	543	0

Note: *From National Highway Safety Administration, Office of Public Affairs, U.S. Department of Transportation. **From National Transportation Safety Board, Washington, DC.

give their estimates and predictions of how many of us will die on the highway during the holiday period.

So logic tells you that you have a significantly greater chance of dying while driving over the holiday weekend than while flying in an airplane over the holiday weekend. Yet many of us still choose to drive. Why? We feel safer. What gives us that feeling of safety? Certainly not our logic and reason, because logic and reason tell us it is safer to fly. It is our sense of control. Behind the wheel of our vehicle, we feel in control. And that feeling of control leads to a reduction in fear, anxiety, and stress.

All of Earth's creatures want control. Teachers and students fit into this category.

LEADERSHIP STYLE DETERMINES PERCEPTION OF CONTROL

Psychologists have been studying classroom leadership styles for decades. From the earliest study, back in 1938, to today, the results remain the same. The leadership style of a teacher can change the behavior of the students in the room as their perception of control changes.

Our first formal look at how leadership styles of teachers affect student behavior came from researcher Kurt Lewin (Lewen, Lippitt, & White, 1939; Lewin & Lippitt, 1938). A refugee from Nazi Germany, Lewin was interested in how leaders could drastically affect the behavior of followers. He used classroom situations as his laboratory setup.

Lewin studied three styles of leaders in a classroom: autocratic, laissez-faire, and democratic. In an autocratic classroom, the teachers made all the decisions and exerted very tight control over student behavior and tasks. In the laissez-faire classroom, teachers gave very little or no guidance, and students had complete freedom. In the democratic classroom, group goals were established, and rules were jointly discussed. While the teacher was the authority in the room, students were given some choice in the direction of the class and the learning.

Lewin's findings and those that have come along since are consistent. You will get the most work out of students with an autocratic classroom leader. You have absolute control, ultimate obedience, and a lot of output. However, you also get very little creativity, cooperation, or problem solving. And perhaps a most important note, once the teacher leaves the room, work ceases completely.

The laissez-faire style of classroom leadership leads to complete chaos. Very little work is completed, and what work is completed is of very poor quality. It should surprise no one that classrooms can't run well without some teacher guidance.

The democratic style of leadership worked the best. While you do not get the quantity of output that you get under an autocratic teacher, the student-generated work that you do get is of the highest quality. Students are most creative and demonstrate excellent problem solving skills, and most interestingly the students work at the same intensity whether the teacher is present or not!

Lewin's finding have been substantiated several times (Berson & Linton, 2005; Lok & Crawford, 2004; Dickson et al., 2003; Veenstra et al., 2003; Emans et al., 2003; Koene et al., 2002; van Engen et al., 2001; Bennis & Nanus, 1997).

An Easy Measure of Leadership

I want to call your attention to one of the last statements made above, as it is one of the easiest ways I've found to tell whether a classroom is under the direction of an autocratic teacher or an authoritative-democratic leader. If the teacher walks out of the room, does the student behavior change? Do students stop working? Change tasks? Break established rules? Do they even notice? In a successfully run student centered, democratic classroom, there frequently is no difference in what's going on whether the teacher is present or not. True leaders create such a strong vision for success in their followers that once the leader leaves, the followers continue down the same path because now the leader's vision is their own vision. As journalist and leadership writer Walter Lippmann said, "The final test of a leader is that he leaves behind him in others the conviction and the will to carry on."

SOLUTION STRATEGIES

So now we come to a place in this book where we need to discuss the subject of our role as leaders in the classroom, because in the classroom the teacher is a coach, a manager, and a leader. What kind of leader should we be, and what exactly is the role of a leader?

Sometimes we are the teacher giving direct instruction, modeling and clarifying content. And sometimes we are the coach on the sideline, facilitating the learning process and trying to stay out of the way. But both of these roles require some strong leadership skills.

Many of us took a course in classroom management during our preservice education. If we really want to move education in the direction of student centeredness and encourage differentiation, then teacher education courses in classroom management should expire. We need to replace them with classroom leadership courses. Strike the term "classroom management" from education because the concept self-perpetuates the problem. The more you manage others, the more they need to be managed. You cannot manage people into being responsible, intrinsically motivated, cooperative people who strive to reach their own personal potential. For that we need classroom leaders.

What is a leader? And what is it that defines a good leader? Most leadership models show us that there are four steps to leadership. Having a vision, sharing that vision, selling the vision, and then facilitating the followers' journey toward that vision.

Leaders First Have a Vision

For a teacher, that vision is an idea of what skills or knowledge you need your students to have. Get an idea of the goals of your curriculum and your personal standards of student excellence. Envision a successful classroom.

Leaders Share Their Vision With Their Followers in Such a Way That It Becomes Everyone's Vision

The next step is the sharing and selling of your vision. You need to have your students or followers "buy into the vision." What's the benefit for getting to our goal. Help students see what is in it for them. Just saying, "can you see yourself at 45, driving the nice car, having the great career?" probably is not going to sell them. If they are 15 or 17 years old, they are most likely not going to buy into that vision. It needs to be shorter term, using the things they value today. Try offering prestige, maybe getting into a good college, popularity, ego, self-efficacy, a sense of pride and accomplishment.

You'll notice that most high school coaches don't motivate players to do well so they can make it to the pros. They coach them to do well so they can win on Saturday or make it to the district playoff THIS season. The long-term goals are presented more subtly.

James Kouzes and Barry Posner (1996) wrote, "There's nothing more demoralizing than a leader who can't clearly articulate why we're doing what we're doing" (p. 46).

PRACTICE ASSIGNMENTS FOR OVERCOMING THIS OBSTACLE

Practical Solution Idea 11.1: Expect excellence.

Remind your students that we are not here to do mediocre work. You as the teacher should expect nothing less than excellence in your students.

> People tend to perform at the level of their own internalized standards. . . . Settling for mediocrity undermines performance because it lowers expectations. . . . Mentors should expect more of their protégés than their protégés typically expect of themselves. This raises their expectations and lifts their performance. (Johnson & Ridley, 2004, p. 7)

Make sure you model the same excellence that you expect.

Practical Solution Idea 11.2: Remove obstacles for your students.

Once your students understand what they are going for, your job is to facilitate, remove obstacles, and sometimes just get out of their way. We often spend so much time coping with problems along our path that we forget why we are on that path in the first place. When that happens we lose sight of our goal or our vision.

So one of your important roles in the classroom is that of a facilitator who helps remove the obstacles that are blocking the path to your students' success. Sometimes that means helping them find alternate ways to learn. Let your students learn in their best learning style; help them challenge themselves and then meet that challenge. Encourage their accomplishments.

Practical Solution Idea 11.3: See yourself sometimes as a coach.

We do not have to be keepers of all knowledge. We do not necessarily have to be smarter than our students in order to help them learn. Did Phil Jackson need to play basketball better than Michael Jordan in order to coach him? Did Richard Callihan have to be a better skater than Tara Lipinski in order to coach her to Olympic gold? Of course, those are really great athletes. What about the ones who aren't superstars? Did Pat Riley have to be a better player than Udonis Haslem of the Miami Heat? Udonis is the lowest-paid player in the National Basketball Association, which tells us that he is probably not one of the best players in the Association. And yet I'm sure even Udonis plays better basketball than Pat Riley, who coached him for the Miami Heat.

So it is not necessary to do more or have greater skill than those you teach. A classroom teacher must sometimes just take the role of coach. Good coaching, like good leadership, takes some practice and some training.

We can learn much from listening to those who have been inspirational athletic coaches:

- Eddie Robinson, the winningest college coach of all time, put it this way: "Coaching is a profession of love. You can't coach people unless you love them."
- Woody Hayes said, "Any time you give a man something he doesn't earn, you cheapen him. Our kids earn what they get, and that includes respect."
- Vince Lombardi said, "The price of success is hard work, dedication to the job at hand, and the determination that whether we win or lose, we have applied the best of ourselves to the task at hand."
- Paul Dietzel said, "Leadership is the ability to lift and inspire."

So caring and love are perhaps the first and most important characteristics of a good teacher who takes the role of coach. It also takes the ability to inspire. Model the learning you are trying to teach. Let students see you learn. Make a goal for yourself on every instructional unit of something you want to learn. Share the goal with your students, and have them check you at the end.

The role of the teacher in an active classroom is that of facilitator, instructor, coach, and leader. Our main purpose is to help students reach their full learning potential, and we should encourage, challenge, and take delight in their learning.

I Don't Know How to Measure My Students' Learning Style

A DESCRIPTION OF THE ISSUE

Students have different styles of learning. Very few people argue this point. The research has been quite robust on the topic; parents and teachers have known it forever, and quite a bit has been written on the topic. So while few people disagree with the concept of learning style, much debate continues as to whether it can really be measured with paper-and-pencil tests. Do students really know their own learning style well enough to accurately share that information with a learning styles inventory?

I don't think we need to wait for resolution of that debate, because a couple of things are already clear. First of all, you don't need to know students' individual learning styles in order to differentiate instruction. And second, it's fairly obvious that today's classrooms are not meeting the diversity.

In his book *Engaging Minds* (2003), David Goslin tells us that our public schools adequately serve only about one-fourth of our students.

> For the most affluent, able and highly engaged students, the American education system is clearly on a par with any educational system in the world. . . . [These] best students are being challenged in all of the ways that critics of our schools have urged that they be challenged. (pp. 7–8)

Goslin puts in writing what most of us already secretly know: for a small, select group of students, the American education system works exceptionally well. What most of us don't want to talk about or address is the other group, the large group that isn't being served by the system. Convention tells us to look the other way; focus on our star successes. We have appeased our conscience with the notion that there is no way to reach *everyone*. It is true that we may never reach and be successful with every last student in our school. But to not reach the vast majority is just not acceptable.

SOLUTION STRATEGIES

It is not necessary to premeasure student learning styles. When given a variety of options, students will discover their own learning style and do so very quickly. This is especially true if you add the accountability factor to the learning, as was mentioned in Chapter 4. Start by awarding some points for the actual learning that occurs on an assignment rather than just the "doing" of the assignments. In other words, value product over process. When students realize that the points are awarded for the learning, not just assignment completion, they will quickly discover their learning style all by themselves.

If you need students to learn vocabulary words, award the points based on the mastery of the vocabulary rather than just the process they used to get there. Offer them several ways or suggestions for how they might learn those words, such as flash cards, a worksheet, or study groups. But have the grading points come from the results of the activity. Offer students credit primarily for what they've learned and not necessarily for how they got there.

As I have tried to emphasize at several points in this book, we put too much value in school on process and not enough on product, when in the real world the scenario is just the opposite. As adults, we rarely get lauded for process, only product. If I have a new job as a waitress in a restaurant and my first assignment is to memorize the menu, my employer will never ask or care about how much time it took me, how nicely my study cards were decorated, how neatly I wrote out my practice sheets at home, or how well I cooperated in the group with the other new waitresses as we memorized the menu prices. What my employer cares about is whether I learned the menu. Period. If I am hired as the new regional sales rep for a pharmaceutical company and my first order of business is to learn the product line, my job success is not based on how hard I studied, what method I used to study, or how nice the poster looked that I created in my office in my attempt to graphically represent the products in my head. In other words, the process I underwent to learn something is rarely valued much, if any, in the adult world. What is valued is simply that I learned it.

What sort of message are we sending our young people when we put more value on the effort, time, and artistic layout of the study tools than on the assessment of the actual learning?

Suppose the unit is Egyptian history. The assignment is to create a poster. Karla's poster of the Egyptian pyramids looks great and displays a wonderful understanding of the use of color and was awarded 15 points, but Karla learned absolutely nothing about Egyptian pyramids in the process.

What's the point? What's the purpose of any assignment? This is what teachers need to ask themselves. And then share that purpose with students. Share with them the objective and then offer some suggestions for ways to learn the objective, but measure the learning. Is the point to learn what Egyptians gave us? The significant contributions of their society? The key components of their culture? What are you trying to learn? I promise you that once you share the objective and let students know you are going to measure the learning, they will take care of evaluating their learning style.

This is not to say that we should never place any value on the process of learning, as that certainly should be applauded and acknowledged, but it should never take precedence over the actual learning.

Along the way, your students may also discover that the way they learn best doesn't match traditional learning strategies. And it sometimes doesn't match the style of their best friend, as was a common scenario in my classroom.

Becky: We have to do one of these vocab assignments. Which one are you doing?

Tara: I'm doing the flash cards. Do you want to work together?

Becky: Yeah, I'll make the cards and you look up the answers.

Tara: OK. Do you think they are all in the glossary?

However, when points were awarded based solely on how many words Becky and Tara could define for me individually, Tara got four out of five, for a score of eight, and Becky knew zero. When this happens, it is time for us to have a talk about friends and learning styles and how they sometimes don't line up. Next time I think Becky ought to try one of the study buddy groups or the worksheet activity.

In the beginning of the year, this scenario may be quite common, but very quickly students discover how to learn and how to choose assignments that give them their best chance of success. And sometimes that means you can't work with your best friend. But sometimes you can, and that is another important life skill.

TAKE A CUE FROM YOUR IEPS

One of the ways differentiation can help address the needs of students is by removing some of the self-defeating obstacles. Differentiation makes it harder for students to directly compare their work with others'. This comparison is a big factor in low perception of ability at the secondary level. If every student is doing pretty much the same assignment every day, it's too easy for students to see their "below average" performance. If they see this on a regular basis, it can be extremely discouraging and can lead to continued low performance.

Teachers have heard that differentiating instruction means that you have to individualize instruction for every student in the room. This doesn't mean you have to predetermine students' learning styles for them and then tailor instruction just for them. In fact, by designating certain assignments for certain students, we often stigmatize the student. We've seen this happen with special education programs. The biggest reason that students leave special education when they hit secondary school is that they don't like the stigma of a "special" program. Students, especially adolescents, like to fit in, blend in, and not be pointed out as having some type of special need.

So be very careful if you do much individual modification. Whenever possible offer those individual modifications to the group. Ideally you want to try to offer whole-class modifications. Just about any individualized education program (IEP) modification can be turned into a whole-class offering.

Exams will be orally read to the student

If you have been told that a student needs exams read aloud, offer an auditory test to the group. You may want to record the test on tape at a listening center or allow any of your students to go down to a resource room where another adult is prepared to read the test. After all, if your school has set up a "special ed" room with an adult to read the test to one particular child from your room, he or she could certainly accommodate a few more.

Photocopied work will be presented on yellow paper or with a yellow overlay

If you have a student who needs material copied on yellow paper, offer materials to the group in a wide variety of colors. Most likely there are other students in your room who would benefit from reading black ink on a paper color other than white. Stock colored overlays in several colors and have them available for anyone to use.

Student will be provided with a note taker for class lectures

If you have a student with an IEP that requires a note taker, offer a written copy of notes to the group. Provide graphic organizers for anyone who wants them. Tape-record your lectures so anyone who needs to relisten at a later date can do so.

Student will have daily class work expectations reduced

If students need a reduction in the amount of work they are given, break assignments up into small pieces and let everyone choose how much they can do. Rather than assign all the practice problems for 20 points, offer the odd-numbered problems for 10 points and the even-numbered problems for 10 points. Students can do both assignments or just one.

These so-called whole-class modifications reduce the stigma on your special needs students and offer some terrific learning strategies to your general population. After all, no one said that special ed modifications can be offered only to special students!

PROVIDE A HOME BASE

One of the things researchers have focused on in designing learning environments for various learning styles is the issue of personal space and a home base. Whether it be at school or at work, or even at play, people feel more comfortable with a well-defined spot that is theirs. In the high school, we tend to think of the locker as the student's home base, and to some extent it is. But it's not sufficient.

Students need a place in the classroom that can be personalized. In elementary school we had cubbies and our own desk with our own pencil box. Once we left elementary school, we had to get used to sharing everything. We certainly couldn't leave our pencils in the desk anymore, because six periods worth of kids used that desk every day.

Try to find a way to allow personalization of space in your classroom. Perhaps you can use something as simple as a pencil box filled with their personal material that stays in the room (secured). Even a file folder they can customize and use to hold their work can offer them a feeling of security. Let them attach photos of their friends and their pets, cartoons, and so forth.

At first glance this seems very elementary school-ish, but look at your classroom desk. Is it personalized? We like to have a space away from home that makes us feel secure and is filled with emotionally familiar things. Those of you who have ever been "traveling teachers" know what I'm talking about. Traveling teachers have no room to call their own.

Instead of a classroom, these teachers get to roll a cart from classroom to classroom throughout the day. How wonderful the day when they finally get a classroom to call their own! Even traveling teachers tend to decorate and personalize their carts.

Remember that a personalized space of your own is an important factor in the formation of one's identity and sense of self-worth. So whether in a work setting or a school setting, having a home base improves behavior, attitude, effort, and a sense of belonging.

By the way, this does not just apply to students. You as a teacher need some private space as well, preferably away from students and possibly close to colleagues. Too many of us are isolated from colleagues, which prevents our creative sharing of ideas. If you don't already have one, look for some space for a department office.

> **Q:** Kathie, I'm afraid that if I offer a written copy of notes to the group, everyone will just take a copy, and no one will actually take their own notes!
>
> **A:** This probably will not happen. Explain the rationale to students, and tell them that they will probably benefit from taking their own notes, but if they are one of those people who find it easier to just listen, then a rough overview can be picked up at the end. Suggest also that they might want to do both—take their own notes and pick up the copy—so they can learn through the comparison.

PRACTICE ASSIGNMENTS FOR OVERCOMING THIS OBSTACLE

So it is not necessary to know or even measure a student's learning style. What is important is that we offer a wide variety of physical, emotional, and academic settings for our students to work in. They will work in their comfort zone.

Practical Solution Idea 12.1: Put more emphasis on the learning rather than the doing.

Practical Solution Idea 12.2: Use individual IEP modifications as cues for making whole-class modifications.

Practical Solution Idea 12.3: Provide an opportunity for students to set up a home base or personal area.

Practical Solution Idea 12.4: Offer a variety of physical learning conditions.

Variation in physical learning conditions includes some of the seating arrangements discussed in previous chapters as well as optional grouping, teaming, and opportunities for social interaction. You may also want to offer the option of full-spectrum lighting rather than just the fluorescent lights common in most classrooms. Incandescent lighting or natural light (if you have windows) can help many students' mental and physical health. Attitude, behavior, and even some reading problems can frequently be improved with full-spectrum lighting.

I Have Neither the Time nor the Funding for All That

A DESCRIPTION OF THE TIME ISSUE

Most teachers find a lecture format easy to prepare. Basically this format requires the teacher to just read, process, and retell. It's a process that most of us are comfortable with and can do easily. Let's face it, most of us don't like to cut, paste, color, or build. It's not our learning style. With the abundance of ancillary materials that now come with publishers' textbooks, a lecture-textbook classroom requires less planning time than a differentiated classroom. Perhaps more importantly, it requires less preparation time in what we find to be an uncomfortable learning style.

I DON'T HAVE THE TIME TO PLAN FOR ALL THAT

Time is a precious commodity. Most of us don't find nearly enough of it during the day. Our time is stretched very thin as we try to prepare for classes, sometimes in four or five different subjects; set up and take down labs and activities; do paperwork; attend faculty meetings, department meetings, and parent meetings; grade papers; meet with students; attend professional development; and try to have a life outside school. To suggest anything that may require additional time is a sure way to invite rejection. Unfortunately many teachers see differentiated instruction as something that requires additional time.

SOLUTION STRATEGIES

Differentiated instruction and planning doesn't necessarily take more time, but it usually takes a different allocation of time. As one successful differentiated classroom teacher told me, "The planning is front loaded. I spend a great deal of time planning the lesson, but it significantly reduces my time during the implementation of the lesson."

Most teachers find this a nice trade-off. So while in the beginning you may spend a large chunk of Sunday afternoon in the planning stages, you should find more time available in your weekdays.

PRACTICE ASSIGNMENTS FOR OVERCOMING THIS OBSTACLE

Practical Solution Idea 13.1: Design assignments and rubrics that are generic.

Most of us struggle with the design of tactile and kinesthetic learning projects as they are the most nontraditional and generally not in our learning style. These kinds of assignments don't have to take a great deal of time to develop. See if you can think of 10–15 different types of assignments that lend themselves easily to modification as the unit topic changes.

For example, "Design a 3 x 5 foot bulletin board display teaching the three most important ideas from our chapter" is an assignment that would work all year. If you make an equally generic grading rubric or set of criteria for that bulletin board, then you can insert this assignment several times during the year. Ideally, you plan it once and use it many times.

Practical Solution Idea 13.2: Share the workload.

As suggested in other chapters, use the buddy system. Team up with a colleague for one unit of differentiated instruction. Each of you plans two or three assignments and grading rubrics that you will share with the other. Now you have five or six assignment choices. Subdivide units or take turns planning units. Have one person design the assignments and one person design the grading rubrics. Meet together again after your lesson has been implemented to share successes and trouble spots.

Practical Solution Idea 13.3: Have your students help with the lesson planning.

Get input from your students on activities they have done in the past, other than listening to lectures and reading, that they found useful and beneficial. You will find as the year goes on that students will become a great resource in helping design lesson plans. Ask them what works and what doesn't work. Give them the learning objective and let them brainstorm various ways they think someone could learn that material. Ask for input on grading rubrics too.

Practical Solution Idea 13.4: Go slow.

Don't think you have to suddenly turn your traditional lecture-textbook, teacher centered classroom into a dynamic student centered discovery zone overnight. Start small. Start with what you are currently doing and try to add one component. Design one differentiated instructional unit per grading term. Next year add one more. Look at this as a long journey, not a mad dash. Go at a pace that is comfortable for you.

A DESCRIPTION OF THE FUNDING ISSUE

There is also a practical side to our dependence on textbooks and lectures. Besides the intrinsic value of the printed word, teachers have relied heavily on textbook and lecture partly because they have limited resources for creative teaching materials. Many teachers have so few materials available that the textbook is the only viable option. But differentiation doesn't require a lot of additional funds.

Creativity is the key to budget shortages when designing lessons for diverse populations. Fortunately teachers are great scroungers. We can scrounge better than just about anyone. And we can scrounge from a variety of sources: colleagues, the in-laws' junk drawer, garage sales, and local merchants all become sources for instructional aids. So put on your creative thinking hat and see how you can use common available materials for alternative learning activities.

SOLUTION STRATEGIES AND PRACTICE ASSIGNMENTS FOR OVERCOMING THIS OBSTACLE

Practical Solution Idea 13.5: Collect reading material.

The first rule of thumb is to use what you already have in the room. This year's textbook, preview copies of texts you have collected, last year's textbook, and any and all ancillary materials that come with textbooks, including software. You can add your old college textbooks and materials as well as any old reference books discarded from the library.

Ask parents to donate college texts they may have that pertain to your subject. Subscribe to some of the trade magazines in your field to keep the reading material current. Use the newspaper and weekly news magazines too. The Internet is always a valuable tool, of course, but keep an assortment of printed materials in the room.

Practical Solution Idea 13.6: Use art supplies.

The usual supply of markers and paints can be supplemented with students' colored pencils and those inexpensive watercolor sets.

Posters don't have to be poster-board size. Cut standard poster board into quarters. Modeling clay is inexpensive. Keep a hefty supply of old textbooks that have been slated for discard. These can go in the art area for students to cut from when making displays.

Practical Solution Idea 13.7: Visit your school district warehouse for surplus materials.

I consider those visits my best treasure hunts. Old tape recorders, listening centers, and even some really old computers can be found in these surplus areas. Not sure how to use some of these surplus materials? Put them in an area and make that the assignment: "Find a way these materials can be used to teach two concepts from this unit." Old computer keyboards are great for this activity. As most of us have learned from our students already, those keys can be popped off the keyboard and rearranged to form new words. Let them do it now in a constructive manner.

Practical Solution Idea 13.8: Use your library.

Borrow materials from your school and public library. Books on tape, videos, DVDs, CDs, and software, as well as reference books, are available through your library. Talk to your media specialists or reference librarians about your topic of study and see what materials they may have that would be useful to you.

TIP: Pour a little plaster of paris in an empty tuna can and set your colored marker set, lid side down, in the wet plaster. Let it harden. You now have a set of markers whose tops won't be lost. The markers all move as a set. When the markers eventually run out, replace the markers only—you use the old caps still in the can.

Solution to Obstacle **14**

I've Been Teaching This Way for Years and It Works

If what you are doing is working beautifully; if you are happy and content in your classroom; if most of your students are successful; if parents, administrators, and your district are pleased with the exceptional results of your teaching, then don't change a thing. Carry on.

If the above statement does not fully describe your situation, you may find some benefit to moving toward differentiation and a more student centered classroom.

A DESCRIPTION OF THE ISSUE

Most of us know teachers who teach very successfully in a textbook-lecture, teacher centered style and have had terrific student achievement doing so. It has been my experience that many of these teachers have somewhat homogeneous classrooms to begin with. In other words, they are the honors English teacher, the advanced placement chemistry teacher, the Spanish IV teacher, or the calculus teacher. From a practical standpoint, these classes are almost a handpicked lot. A student taking AP chemistry has already demonstrated success in a traditional classroom. Students taking Mr. Taylor's honors English class do so as an elective, knowing full well the teaching style and expectations of that class, and they are up to the journey. This is not to say that these teachers are not excellent teachers, but we need to recognize that oftentimes the homogeneity of these classes removes any real pressure or great need for differentiation.

How would these same teaching styles work in a "Statue of Liberty" classroom? That's the name I give those classes that are generally required courses that all students must take and pass to graduate. I call them Statue of Liberty classrooms as I sometimes feel that I stand at the door with my torch, proclaiming as Lady Liberty does:

> Give me your tired, your poor,
>
> Your huddled masses yearning to breathe free,
>
> The wretched refuse of your teeming shore.
>
> Send these, the homeless, tempest-tost to me.
>
> I lift my lamp beside the golden door!

Most of my teaching experience has been in these heterogeneous, mixed-ability classrooms full of the "huddled masses yearning to breathe free." For teachers like me, the need to differentiate is greater than for some of our colleagues with more homogeneous classrooms, where the learning styles of the students more closely resemble those found in a college lecture hall.

My advice to teachers is always "If what you are doing now is working, don't change anything." Obviously if your current teaching method is working for nearly all your students and both you and they are happy with it, why would you change?

Or, as the saying goes, "If it ain't broke, don't fix it."

But even those of you with very homogeneous classrooms of high-ability readers and auditory learners may find your students could benefit from some variation in teaching style. For many of the reasons mentioned in this book, especially in Chapter 17, on college preparation, students can benefit from exposure to new ways of learning (Do & Schallert, 2004; Tervaniemi & Hugdahl, 2003; Winebrenner, 2000).

SOLUTION STRATEGIES

Homogeneous classrooms can benefit from differentiation too. There are many differentiation strategies that will enhance the learning and memory recall of information for all students, even our brightest and most school abled. The more you can let students play around with ideas and concepts, the better chance they have for real learning to take place. Playing around with concepts is important in reaching those brain areas responsible for more complex thinking (Doyle, 1983; Perry, 1998; Blumenfeld et al., 1991; O'Reilly & Rudy, 2000; Lodewyk & Winne, 2005).

The basic brain structures involved in learning are the hippocampus and the neocortex. Both of these are heavily involved in learning new tasks and material. The hippocampus lies underneath the cortex of the brain and processes things very quickly. It uses completely separate representations to code facts and details into memory. It is very much involved in the rote memorization and recall of material. The neocortex, however, is a higher area of the brain and takes much longer to process information. It overlaps categories, finds cross-references, and attempts to find patterns and relationships and to analyze the structure of information. These two areas account for the difference between memorizing something and learning it. Students can memorize things very quickly, but to really learn something takes time as the neocortex plays with the concepts and attempts to find how new information can relate and apply to previously learned information.

PRACTICE ASSIGNMENTS FOR OVERCOMING THIS OBSTACLE

Give your students opportunities to play with concepts. Use hands-on activities, group discussion and debate, individual and group projects, and alternate ways to look at ideas. All of these things will help move the students from merely memorizing discreet concepts to true understanding and the ability to find use for new concepts.

Practical Solution Idea 14.1: Elicit emotion.

Memory and recall are also greatly affected by emotion and emotional experiences. When you think back on your school days, what is your most memorable experience? Ask three or four people you meet today to relate to you their most memorable school experience.

Lisa, who has been out of school for 10 years, remembered this:

> I remember my 10th grade year, when I won the award at my school for best supporting actress. That was a really big deal for me as I was always this real skinny kid who everyone picked on, so that was really something for me that day.

Maggie, who has been out of school for 35 years, recalled this:

> My most memorable experience was in first grade. It was the first day of school, and I went to a Catholic school. We had uniforms, plaid skirt and knee socks. My mother had bought me a new pair of brown leather shoes for the school year. By mid-morning my feet were getting so hot inside the shoes in those heavy socks, so I slid them out of my shoes and set them on the top so my feet could cool off. Well, Sister (the nun teaching the class) saw my feet out of my shoes, and she took my shoes and threw them in the trash can. "Let this be a lesson to you not to remove your shoes in school." I was

horrified. I spent the whole day having to walk around in my socks. I was so worried over what my mother was going to say as those were brand new shoes, and we had eight kids in our family, so there wasn't much money. I wasn't sure if she would be able to buy me other shoes. At the end of the day, the nun came and told me I could go get my shoes out of the trash. I still remember leaning way over into that trashcan, digging through all the day's garbage, orange peels and milk cartons, leftover sandwiches, and pencil shavings, trying to get to my shoes. I'll never forget that day.

Kevin, who has been out of school for 28 years, told the following story:

I was in I think sixth grade, and I had written a paper on Louis Pasteur. It was about a boy who was trying to solve a problem, and in the end he met up with Pasteur to solve the problem. I guess it was like a historical fiction story. My teacher reported to my Mom that in all her years of teaching, she'd never seen anyone write so well in the sixth grade. I think that's when I started thinking of myself as a writer.

Paul, who has been out of school for 33 years, recalled this:

I remember a day in English class during my junior year of high school. I don't remember the teacher's name, but she was pretty strict and regimented. But one day she brought in a record with the song "Don't Rock the Boat." It was a little 45-rpm record, and she played it on the old school turntable. She played it over and over again, and we had to write the lyrics. "Rock the boat, Don't rock the boat baby, rock the boat, . . . don't tip the boat over . . . rock the boat, rock the boat." We were studying poetry, I think, and she was trying to show us how you could repeat things over and over in a poem to make a point. All I remember is that I thought that was so cool that this English teacher would bring in a contemporary song that we teens were listening to and actually play it during English class. It was so out of the ordinary. Whenever I think of my high school days, that song still pops into my head.

What do all these stories have in common? They are all memories of events that had significant emotions attached to them. They are stories of events that were funny, sad, scary, motivating, or so far from the standard conduct that they were surprises. We have a lot of days in school, but the ones we carry with us (sometimes for life) are those episodic memories that have emotional components.

Episodic memories are those memories that become our autobiography. They are the recordings of our daily lives. (This is a different memory system from semantic memory, which is the system that records things we intentionally set out to learn, such as the capitals of all the states or how to factor polynomials.) We have no control, really, over our episodic memory. Things just go in there whether we want them to or not. Most of us can recall what we were wearing yesterday, the weather from last Saturday, and probably where we spent our last birthday. We did not set out to store these memories. They just went in. Some of these become crystallized and can be recalled years later; some just fade away. For example, you may recall the weather of last Saturday, but do you remember the weather from six Saturdays ago? Probably not. One of the things that really helps crystallize an episodic memory is emotion. You may be able to tell me the weather on the Saturday you were married many years ago. Or you may be able to tell me the weather the day your child was born or the day you buried a loved one. The emotions that occur during these events can help cement them into our heads.

Practical Solution Idea 14.2: Conduct investigations.

Take advantage of this natural learning process in the brain. In education we call teaching through the episodic memory hands-on learning, or experiential learning. Remember that episodic memories are beyond one's control. So the biggest advantage to hands-on learning in your classroom is that ideas and concepts will go into your students' heads whether they want them to or not. That's quite an advantage for a teacher.

The disadvantage to hands-on learning is that it tends to be time consuming. But fortunately the brain is really good about cross-connecting our two memory systems. So if you can attach a lot of semantic information to an episodic experience, you have a very powerful and effective learning system going. And of course the real key is to create that episodic experience in a highly aroused emotional state. Think weird, novel, or funny. Anything designed to break the monotony of the school day will help create an aroused emotional state in your students.

Labs don't have to involve expensive equipment; they really just need to be novel, hands on, and designed to expand on a concept that students are learning about. And labs don't have to be confined to the science classroom. Just about every subject and discipline has areas that can be investigated.

Practical Solution Idea 14.3: Use modern art.

Modern brain research is showing us that at no time in life is art more important to us than during adolescence. Art feeds a region of the brain known as the hypothalamus, a primitive region responsible for primitive survival needs. This area is at its most active during adolescence due to the hormones associated with puberty, especially testosterone. These hormones really excite and act on the hypothalamus.

So does art. Art is just a creative expression of emotion. You may not have thought about it, but the age group that spends the most time, energy, and money on art is the adolescent. And of course their favorite art form is music. Anyone who raises a teen knows they have that art attached to their heads 24/7!

Art feeds the hypothalamus, and teens are hypothalamus-driven beings. The two go hand in hand. Our love for art develops during this period. If you don't believe me, ask yourself what kind of music you today would prefer to listen to on the radio. My guess is, given a choice, most of us tune into the music that was popular when we were adolescents.

So take advantage of this avenue too. Look at modern art. I'm referring to the art forms that your students enjoy. It's hard, I know. Our poor old adult brains, with our strong prefrontal cortex and less active hypothalamus, just can't feel the soul in much of today's art. That's okay; use it anyway. Find ways to tie your teaching objectives into the music, film, literature, and other artistic expression of today's teens. Now you will be speaking their language.

One of the best things about using their art is that you probably don't need funds to purchase it. Your students have plenty of the materials and are more than happy to share, borrow, and debate the arts.

You don't need to center your entire curriculum around their art, but include it and tie it in where you can. The experience will be novel, something they can relate to, and an enjoyable learning activity. Some math concepts, literature analysis, physical laws, foreign language, and life science issues can be cross-connected to teen art forms.

There's No Support for It at My School

Lack of support from colleagues and administrators may frequently be a case of different perspectives, different perceptions, and different mental models. Sometimes one person's perceptions don't match another person's. Our mental models are different.

My wonderful husband of 25 years may not be the most attentive individual, and sometimes that leads to embarrassing and confused moments, such as one we had last Christmas. My husband's mother sends simple Christmas gifts for the family weeks ahead of Christmas. To keep the gifts from getting lost among the other things under the tree on Christmas morning, it has become a family tradition of sorts to open them when they arrive. My hope is that this might shed a special light on the gifts. Last year each of the children received a book in our Grandmother Christmas box. I received a handmade Christmas tree skirt designed to fit around the base of our Christmas tree. It was beautifully pieced and quilted with little gold tinkle bells along the scalloped edge. I was truly delighted with it because after 25 years, it was nice to have something besides a white bedsheet draped around the Christmas tree. So I was thrilled to place the handmade tree skirt around our tree. We placed all the gifts around it.

On Christmas eve, Grandma called to see whether the gifts had arrived. My husband, caught a bit off guard as he hadn't been paying attention when we opened the box, held his hand over the receiver and whispered to me across the room, "What did she send?"

"Books."

"What?"

"Books for the kids" was my shouted whisper.

So into the receiver my husband spoke with enthusiasm to his mother, "Oh, the children's books are wonderful. Just perfect. They really enjoyed them." . . . mm hm. "Kole's???" I saw the mimed panic as questioning eyes pleaded to me across the kitchen.

"She sent him a book on dinosaurs" came my shout-whisper.

Again into the phone, "Oh, Kole's was perfect. How did you know he loves dinosaurs?"

In my attempt to continue to help my poor inattentive husband, I added,

"And tell her I love the Christmas tree skirt."

"The what?"

"The Christmas tree skirt! She made me a Christmas tree skirt."

"Oh." Into the phone, "and Kathie just loves the Christmas tree skirt. . . . Yes, she thinks it's beautiful. In fact, she's wearing it right now!"

A DESCRIPTION OF THE ISSUE

Different mental models can sometimes leave all parties a bit confused. This is truly the case with differentiated instruction. Many people hear the term "differentiated instruction," and what leaps to mind is either a room of chaos or a kindergarten room full of centers teaching primitive or watered-down concepts.

The only differentiated models many of us have seen are those designed for elementary classes, where students move from the alphabet center to the math manipulative center and then to the play kitchen. Or perhaps just the thought of letting students move around the room doing whatever they want makes the hair stand up on the back of your neck. But differentiated instruction doesn't have to be noisy, chaotic, or based on centers. It can be done in an infinite numbers of ways, and you can maintain whatever degree of control, quiet, and organization you need. But a differentiated classroom may not look like the traditional high school classroom, and for that reason you do need a support system.

If your administration is working from a mental model of a learning environment that is different from yours, you may need to gain some collegial support first and then bring a united front to the administrators' door to help them see what you are doing.

If no one at your school is doing any type of differentiation, it can certainly be tough to go it alone. Trying something new has its risks, and without support many teachers are afraid to take that risk. Worse than a lack of support, sometimes you may even encounter resistance by administrators, colleagues, or both.

I recently had an e-mail from a teacher who had been trying to make her classroom very student centered and to differentiate as many assignments as she could. She reported various parent complaints at parent-teacher night, parent complaints to her administrator, and administrator complaints to her. Despite requests that her administrator visit her classroom, there were no visits. Administrator and parent discussions went on, and in one instance a student was actually pulled out of her class and moved to another teacher's classroom. I could feel the frustration and probably even some tears on the other end of that e-mail. Fear: it's probably one of the biggest reasons teachers won't attempt differentiation in high school. Perhaps the title of this chapter should really be "The Fear Factor."

We have all seen those great inspirational posters and banners that read "Stand up for what you believe is right, even if you stand alone." I saw one just the other day in the cafeteria of my son's middle school. It's a wonderful motto: very inspirational and looks good on the walls. Yet it is one of those things that works great as a theory but can be downright impossible in reality. No one wants to stand alone. We humans are conformists by nature. We want to fit in. We want to belong. Sure, we like to be unique in some fashion, but for the most part we want to look and act within the standards of normal behavior in our peer group (see Sidebar and Bond & Smith, 1996).

Soloman Asch did the classic study on conformity in the early 1950s. Asch asked young adults to be volunteer subjects in a study designed to test visual discrimination—their ability to make accurate visual judgments. If you were one of his subjects, he brought you in a room and seated you near the end of a table full of other young adults who you didn't know. A card was presented to the group with lines on it like this:

LINE A   Group B: X   Y   Z

The question posed to the group was which of the lines in group B looks to be closest in length to the line A? Each person in the group responded in turn. Surprisingly though, each person said that line Z looked closest in length when you in fact think it's pretty obvious that it is line Y that is the correct answer. After five or six people before you respond with the line Z response, it's now your turn to answer. What do you say?

If you are like most of the subjects in Asch's experiment, you will respond also with "line Z" even though you really believe that to be the wrong answer. Why? You don't want to be perceived as peculiar, or you may even start to doubt your own perceptions. But whatever the reason, more than 75 percent of us conform in those situations.

What is even more interesting about this study is that Asch went on to try different scenarios. How big did the group have to be before we would "conform?" What happens if we have other dissenters in the group? Asch found answers to both these questions. The group size? Somewhere between just three and four! And the number of others we need on our "team"—just one! "Yes, regardless of the size of the group, if just ONE other person at the table chooses Line Y before we do, we have the confidence to stand by our beliefs" (Asch, 1955, 1956).

Asch's comments on the conclusions of his study can be found in his quote:

"The tendency to conformity in our society is so strong that reasonably intelligent and well-meaning young people are willing to call white black. This is a matter of concern. It raises questions about our ways of education and about the values that guide our conduct" (1955, p. 34).

This study has been replicated many times since the 1950s and while there is a little variation from country to country, we as humans still remain a fairly conformist animal. (See Bond & Smith, 1996.)

SOLUTION STRATEGIES

Because the teacher centered classroom is the norm in most high schools, a teacher is hesitant to branch out alone with student centered instruction. To go it alone almost guarantees failure; failure not because the methodology isn't right or good, but failure simply due to a lack of collegial or administrative support.

Don't do that to yourself. Before beginning any change in classroom philosophy, get a buddy or, better yet, a small group of buddies. Ever try a new exercise program alone? Ever try it with a partner? Which is easier? It's always easier with a support system. The same is true here. Find a colleague, preferably in your own building, who is interested in also trying to design and implement some differentiated strategies. It doesn't have to be someone in your same teaching discipline or even your same department. If you can't find someone in your school, look to a colleague in a neighboring high school. You just need someone you can form an emotional bridge with to help you weather any storms.

Use this person or group to help generate ideas, get feedback on newly designed lessons before you implement them, and most important, share ideas with after lessons have been implemented. A small book-study group or teacher-directed study group works great. If you can find mutual time to meet once a week, terrific. If you can't always meet face to face, make a phone contact or e-mail contact. Remember, you need only one person. Studies on conformity have been going on for decades, and what is fascinating is the strength of conviction we get from just one confidant. Never underestimate the power of a support person.

PRACTICE ASSIGNMENTS
FOR OVERCOMING THIS OBSTACLE

Practical Solution Idea 15.1: Put together a team of colleagues to work on differentiated instruction.

Really make it a working team, with various roles assigned which all support the joint goals of the group. We can borrow ideas from the business community about what makes an effective team for change (Skopec & Smith, 1997). A good working team includes some essential elements and follows certain ideals. Try to include these essential elements in your team to make good progress toward differentiated instruction.

- Include diversity of skill, expertise, and personality.

  This means you may want to include teachers of varying grade levels, subjects, and years of experience. You may want to bring in some middle-grade teachers as well.

- Take some time to form a good relationship among the people.

    You may want to start by having just an informal meeting in a relaxed atmosphere away from school.

- Team members must show mutual support.

    Make sure everyone on the team wants to be there and shares the vision and goals.

- Team members must expect to be influenced (sometimes deeply) by others on the team.

    You want people who are open to new ideas and are not afraid to challenge some old personal beliefs that may result from close team work.

- Everyone will come with an open mind and an open attitude about change and compromise.
- Be ready to assist your teammates without judging them so that everyone is open to taking risks.

    Be vigilant about personal attacks or quick negative reactions to any member's ideas or suggestions.

- Knowledge is used for shared power, not personal power.

    This can be a difficult issue for many people, so be aware. Encourage the free sharing of information, expertise, research, and knowledge.

- Don't let any feelings of superiority separate you and your team from the rest of the faculty.

    All educators share common goals, and while we may take different paths and dedicate different amounts of time and energy to those goals, we are all members of the larger faculty community at our schools.

My District Requires Me to Follow a Prescribed Text

A DESCRIPTION OF THE ISSUE

Textbooks are an integral part of school. Students look for them on the first day of school. Parents use their existence as a measure of how well their school is doing. Districts budget more money for textbooks than for all other teaching aids combined. Textbooks are probably here to stay for the foreseeable future. However, there are reasons that teachers should, at the very least, supplement textbooks with additional or alternate information and sources.

TEXTBOOK OPTIONS CAN CREATE MORE EFFECTIVE READERS

When you use a variety of textbooks, you increase the likelihood that one will spark the interest of a particular student, a key ingredient in successful reading. Reading comprehension involves more than simply decoding words. It involves motivation. Students must feel some motivation to learn through reading, or else academic success will be limited, particularly for high school students (Dolezal et al., 2003; Reynolds & Symons, 2001; Shaywitz, 2003; Stipek, 2002).

Learning through reading involves three key processes: phonological and decoding skills, motivation, and engagement. As high school teachers, we frequently do not need to assist our students with the phonological and decoding process, but the most effective teachers are those who make a significant effort to support student motivation and engagement in reading. If students "want" to understand the material, they will process the material more deeply (McCrudden et al., 2005).

Modern research in reading has shown us that simply having a textbook that matches the reading level of your students is not enough for real learning. If we expect our students to glean usable information from a text, we must include the five keys to motivating students for effective textbook reading:

- Before reading, the students must have an understanding of the content goals.
- The students should have a choice of texts.
- The students perceive their textbooks as interesting.
- There is significant social collaboration during reading.
- Small-group instruction should be used as support for the reading.

When trying to motivate and engage your students in a textbook, take into consideration that both cognitive skills and emotional issues are involved in engagement. Most of us have been trained in helping students engage cognitive skills. We have been taught, for example, to help students activate background knowledge with the use of questioning and summarizing techniques and graphic organizers.

But students who successfully gain knowledge and understanding through reading are those students in classrooms where the teacher also helps with the emotional component of reading engagement. There are good motivational practices that teachers can use to help students with reading. These include things like using content goals, providing hands-on activities, offering students choice, using interesting texts, and encouraging social collaboration during reading instruction.

A VARIETY OF READING MATERIALS
KEEPS INFORMATION UPDATED

Many texts may be outdated. Some are outdated almost as fast as they are published. Many of us teach in fields where new information changes ideas almost weekly. Subjects such as social studies, geography, the sciences, art, music, technology, business, and industrial arts all must use supplemental materials in order to keep up with changing issues and new information in the field.

We are all aware of the length of time it takes to write, edit, revise, publish, and market a text. In fields such as computer technology, genetic science, and world geography, much has occurred and changed during the years it took to move a textbook from the author's writing to your classroom.

Another reason for supplemental or multiple texts is one that is rarely discussed in department meetings. Textbooks are often full of inaccuracies and information that is just plain wrong. In 2000, *Forbes* magazine printed a very unsettling exposé of the ongoing errors and accuracy problems with school texts. The story began when a retired physicist volunteered to teach eighth grade earth science and found dozens and dozens of errors in the state-adopted textbook. Errors of fact, interpretation, and omission were found throughout the text. Further investigation found allegations of text errors that had gone without correction for years despite having been reported to the textbooks' publishers (McClintick, 2000).

It may come as a surprise to many teachers and students that the authors listed on the cover of their textbook may have had little, if anything, to do with the words printed on the pages within. The scientists, historians, and authors listed are there mainly to lend credence and help sell the textbooks. Most textbooks are actually written by a team of staff writers working for the publishing houses and using notes, directions, and standards drawn up by textbook committee members from California and Texas, the two lead states for text adoptions.

Is it any wonder, then, that many teachers feel a strong need to provide additional or supplemental sources of information? This is not to say that textbooks have little value in the classroom. On the contrary, a good textbook can be an excellent source of information and a good overview of the subject. But keep in mind that while most textbooks go through a fairly elaborate editorial process, there are significant differences among texts in the political and social interpretations they convey.

A VARIETY OF TEXTS MAKES THE INFORMATION AVAILABLE TO MORE STUDENTS

Many textbooks are adopted based on a grade level readability number. In other words, a textbook rated at a 10th grade readability level is generally thought to be best for 10th graders. Many educators and text adoption committee members may not be familiar with what readability levels actually represent. A textbook with a 10th grade readability level means that *50 percent* of 10th graders can read and comprehend this textbook *with teacher assistance*. That's very different from saying that the majority of 10th graders can read and understand this textbook through independent reading.

So if you are using your textbook for in-class reading and discussion, pausing periodically to point out the new words, relate concepts to the photos on the page, and so on, then a 10th grade readability text is probably appropriate for your 10th grade class. But that is not how most high school teachers use their textbook. Most of us assign passages from the text as independent reading. "Read sections 1 and 2 from Chapter 23 tonight for a quiz tomorrow." If that's how you are using your textbook, then you probably should be using one at a readability level one or two grades below your teaching grade level. (If you teach 11th grade, then use a 9th grade readability textbook, for example.)

Q: Kathie, how can I determine the readability level of my department-adopted textbook?

A: There are several ways you can establish the readability of a textbook and/or see if your text is a good fit with your students. One of the easiest is to have students take a CLOZE test using random passages from the text. Simply copy several paragraphs, leaving a blank in place of every fifth word. Students need to make their best guess as to the missing word. You can set your own criteria, but generally if the student can get 60 percent to 70 percent of the answers correct, the text is a good fit for independent reading. You can download a free piece of software that will generate cloze tests from your text at: http://drott.cis.drexel.edu/clozeproze.htm.

If you are simply trying to determine the grade level readability of your text, you can use the standard Fry formula. Some publishers will give you the readability information, but you may want to run this quick test yourself just to be sure.

Find three 100-word passages from your textbook. Find samples where the text has a lengthy narrative flow, and use samples from the beginning, middle, and end of the textbook. Now read the text out loud, counting (make slash marks on scratch paper) the syllables in the 100-word passage. You may want to use more than three passages, but that's the minimum. Average the syllable counts you get, and you have a number that you can then plug into a chart to see the readability. A quick search on the Internet will give you a PDF of a Fry Readability chart, or you can go right to the source, *The Reading Teacher's Book of Lists,* by Edward Fry himself (Englewood Cliffs, NJ: Prentice Hall).

SOLUTION STRATEGIES

So, armed with your solid reasons for wanting multiple or at least supplemental texts, it's fairly easy to justify your need to your department or district. There is a limitless supply of supplemental reading material. And while you are looking, make sure you gather a wide range of sources to meet the needs of your diverse group of learners.

We can certainly see that the motivational reading strategies presented above are best done in a differentiated classroom. Classrooms that use both cognitive and motivational emotional strategies have been shown to give us our best learning and student performance for later recall on standardized tests (Guthrie et al., 2004; Pressley, 2000; Wigfield & Tonks, 2004).

PRACTICE ASSIGNMENTS
FOR OVERCOMING THIS OBSTACLE

Practical Solution Idea 16.1: Set goals.

There has to be a goal for the reading. Use a multitude of instructional strategies to help students understand the objective of the reading and set goals for their learning.

Practical Solution Idea 16.2: Add a variety of accountability strategies to the reading.

Students who do not expect to be held accountable for learning from a text are more likely to process the text superficially than students do who read in preparation for some type of test or quiz. Research shows us that students use different reading strategies depending on what they will ultimately be expected to do with the information. They use one set of reading strategies (memorization and elaboration) if they are going to have a test, a different set of strategies (monitoring) if they will need to participate in a discussion, and a completely different set of strategies (organization) if they will have to do a written summary (Braten & Samuelstuen, 2004). Here again, we see the advantages of a differentiated classroom.

Practical Solution Idea 16.3: Issue students a textbook.

Every school I have ever taught in had a department- or district-adopted text. Textbooks are a big issue with schools and with parents. In fact, "one student, one textbook" seems to be a fundamental measuring stick by which parents determine whether their school is doing all right. Nothing causes more outright rebellion by parents than a school that doesn't have "enough books to go around." Rather than try to change this deeply held belief, I've always found it easiest to just go ahead and issue every student a textbook.

At the beginning of the year, I would issue each student a text, with directions to take it home and leave it there. This solved two problems. First, parents were happy to see their children had their own textbook. Secondly, I knew students had a book at home that they could refer to for homework or for work during an absence or to review for a test. We never had to worry that the book was at school when it should have been home or that it was at home when it should have been at school.

In our classroom, however, we used a wide variety of textbooks, and they were used as references, resources, and supplemental material. Occasionally I would offer readings and assignments out of the adopted text, but students could use the copies I kept in the room, or they could complete that assignment from home. My class sets didn't wander off, either, because students knew they had their own copy at home.

Practical Solution Idea 16.4: Use the newspaper every day in your room.

Encourage students to find current events in your subject. Music, science, math, art, history, technology, and sports are all represented on a daily basis in the newspaper. Have students read a story in two different papers by two different writers. Compare and contrast the two stories. Have them read a story and watch the news coverage on television. Compare and contrast the stories.

Practical Solution Idea 16.5: Let them compare text accounts to primary accounts.

Have students read an account in your text and then go back into newspaper archives to read the actual account of the day. Many students are not even aware of the existence of microfiche and other archived news records in their public library. That "old" technology is novel to them, and believe it or not, just cranking the film around on the spool while reading and searching can help a kinesthetic learner.

Practical Solution Idea 16.6: Use groups to ensure a variety of sources.

Assign students to groups where each student will gather information on a topic from a different source: one will read the textbook account, one will do an Internet search, one will watch a video documentary, and one will search out a primary source. Each student takes notes on the key issues, and then they all meet back together as a team to compare notes.

Practical Solution Idea 16.7: Mix and match text reading with supplemental material.

Require all students to read the chapter summary from the text. Now offer a choice for the remainder of the assignment. They can then go back and read the entire chapter, or they can watch a video on the topic, or they can do an Internet search and compose an annotated bibliography of the sites they've found.

Parents Expect Lecture Format in High School for College Prep

I n the Western world, we may be called teachers or leaders. In some Eastern societies, we are called masters. But if we venture into some Tao philosophy, we find the idea that one needs a master only in the beginning. For a true master is one who helps you find the true master within.

A DESCRIPTION OF THE ISSUE

Parents expect a lecture format in high school because most parents expect or at least hope their kids will go to college, and they know that their child will most likely encounter a lecture format in college. If Johnny is to do well in college, he better start learning how to listen to a lecture and take notes.

This parental thinking is partly true. Most college classes, as we are all aware, are based heavily on a lecture format. But think about the learning of that material. Most of the learning and preparation for exams does not occur in the lecture hall. It occurs outside that classroom. The purpose of good note taking was so you could get enough of the important ideas down on paper for later. Later was the learning part. That's when you took the information, pulled it off the page, and manipulated it in your mind in such a fashion that it made sense. You made relationships out of the information so that you could store it, apply it, or later demonstrate it. Lucky the individual who knew some creative ways to do that. Lucky the student who came from a differentiated high school environment that exposed him or her to a wide array of strategy choices.

Differentiating instruction is not just about helping kids learn in their own way; it's also about teaching them options, flexibility, and creativity. All of these skills are a necessary component for survival in a variety of post–high school avenues, especially college. Unfortunately a rigorous college-prep curriculum often neglects to foster and develop good independent learning skills. One of the leading authorities on personal autonomy and student learning, Edward Deci (1995), writes,

> In a way, it is all quite ironic. Parents, politicians, and school administrators all want students to be creative problem-solvers and to learn material at a deep, conceptual level. But in their eagerness to achieve these ends, they pressure teachers to produce. The paradox is that the more they do that, the more controlling the teachers become, which, as we have seen so many times, undermines intrinsic motivation, creativity, and conceptual understanding in the students. The harder the teachers are pushed to get results, the less likely it is that the important results will be forthcoming. (p. 158)

Flexibility and adaptability are two of the most significant life skills we can help students gain. If they never see different ways to learn, how can they know them? If you've learned math facts only from books or problem sets on worksheets, how would you know that perhaps a three-dimensional view may actually help you visualize a solution strategy for a difficult problem? I can make vocabulary flashcards but personally have never found them helpful learning tools. But I never thought to learn vocabulary in any other way because flashcards were the norm. I was amazed, as an adult, to watch a student make cartoons for vocabulary words. Each word was illustrated in such a way as to explain the definition. It had never occurred to me to try different ways because I had not been exposed to many.

Can you imagine the advantage of a classroom where students get to actually see classmates learn the same vocabulary words but through four or five different avenues? Some students may draw cartoons, some make humorous bumper stickers, some use a computer matching program, and some students use flash cards.

DIFFERENTIATED READING STRATEGIES HELP PREPARE STUDENTS FOR COLLEGE LEARNING

From about the fourth grade on, students are expected to glean a tremendous amount of "learning" from textbooks. At no place is this a greater expectation than in college. All of us, as college graduates, know how important reading skills are to a college student. Competent readers will generally survive college. Struggling readers will have a very difficult time.

Therefore, if your goal is to function as a college preparatory school, one of the key things you should be focusing on is helping your students improve their ability to gain a deep understanding of concepts through reading. Differentiated instruction allows a teacher to do that. In fact, if you are not differentiating, your students are at a disadvantage in terms of effective reading strategy skills.

The research on competent reading and reading for learning is quite robust (Guthrie et al., 2004; Dolezal et al., 2003; Stipek, 2002; Ozgungor & Guthrie, 2004; National Reading Panel, 2000). Good reading comprehension involves motivation. Simply decoding words is not sufficient. Students must feel some motivation to learn through reading, or else their academic success is limited. Learning through reading, as we saw in Chapter 16, involves three key ingredients:

- phonological/decoding skills
- engagement
- motivation

The more you can help your students gain skills in all three of these areas, the better they will be prepared for college.

Differentiated instruction can help your students particularly in two of these three areas. Effective teachers are those who make a significant effort to support student motivation and engagement in reading (Dolezal et al., 2003). At the high school level, this aspect of reading is even more important because we can assume that many of our students have some mastery of decoding and phonological processing. What we tend to forget, though, is that we must still focus on those other two keys of reading—motivation and engagement.

Increasing reading motivation in particular is important. If students *want* to understand the material, they will process that material at a deeper level.

We are all aware that a significant number of our students come into our high school classrooms and are unable to even decode the words of our text without a lot of struggle. It is no secret that many of our students are not good readers at the basic, phonological level. But we have covered those poor readers or nonreaders in earlier chapters. Here I want to focus on the fairly competent readers, those who have basically mastered the mechanics of reading. Teachers can easily feel no need to differentiate instruction for these students because the vast majority of them can in fact read the adopted class textbook.

For these students, though, teachers need to focus on those two other key ingredients of successful reading—motivation and engagement. Students who can strengthen these learning skills in high school will have a significant advantage in college. The research on effective reading shows that teachers, especially high school teachers, can do much to help students learn to be engaged readers and to help motivate them in their reading.

SOLUTION STRATEGIES

If your parents demand lecture and note-taking practice, that's great. Include it. For college-bound students it will be great preparation. Most of us are aware that note taking is a learned skill and one many students struggle with. So note-taking strategies are an excellent use of class time for college-prep high schools.

But don't stop there. Teach your students what to do with those notes. How do you take them and turn them into learning? What are some ways these can be manipulated or played with? What are some options for meaningful application?

And don't forget about those students who may never be successful listeners and note takers. What about them? Can you help them learn to compensate? Are there other strategies for learning the material that they might try?

Communicate with your parents. Let them know the "method to your madness." Keep some lecture in your day. If you have a room full of auditory learners, it may even be the vast majority of your class period. (You should still plan some accommodation for the serious nonauditory learner.) Perhaps your focus can be on differentiating the homework or labs. Offer variety in how students present their view of the ideas and concepts. Give them a variety of ways to manipulate that information on the page into useful ideas that can be recalled, applied, and redesigned.

Let students know that there are other ways to learn. Explain a variety of note-taking strategies. Perhaps have them use an audiotape if note taking distracts their attention from the lecture (I fit in this category and was one of those college students who rarely wrote down more than the key terms). What do they do if they miss a lecture? Will copying a classmate's notes help them recover? Somewhat, but probably not completely. They may need to look over a few people's notes. They may need to do some supplemental reading. Give options for makeup work so students can see a variety of strategies. Offer a variety of note-taking planners, outlines, and graphic worksheets for them to choose from when taking notes.

Encourage students to try some of each and see which ones work best for them.

Note Planner - Outline Format

I. Main Idea: _____

   A. Subpart _____

   B. Subpart _____

      1. details _____

      2. details _____

II. Main Idea: _____

   A. Subpart _____

   B. Subpart _____

   C. Subpart _____

III. Main Idea: _____

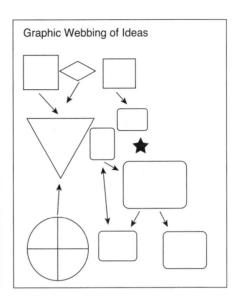

Graphic Webbing of Ideas

My comments, thoughts, questions, ideas

Teacher's Outline

I.

  A.

  B.

    1.

    2.

II.

  A.

  B.

  C.

III.

  A.

    1.

    2.

    3.

  B.

An engaged reader is an active reader. Here are some research-based, established strategies for reading engagement:

1. While reading, activate prior knowledge

Before students read a text assignment, have them think about and discuss what they already know about the topic. You may also want to encourage them to stop frequently during their reading to relate the new concepts to background knowledge. This can even be an assignment done in small reading groups.

2. While reading, use questioning strategies

Have your students generate questions while reading. You may want to have them write some down or reread a passage and respond to some peer-generated questions.

3. While reading, be searching for information

Give students a reason for reading. Pose questions or discuss the purpose ahead of time. These may be generated during your prereading discussion that activated prior knowledge. You want students to feel they are reading not just for vague familiarity with the material but in order to find an answer to a problem or question.

4. Summarize what you just read

Have students stop periodically and summarize the key concepts. This can be done in their heads or by putting the summaries in writing.

5. Use graphic organizers

Encourage students to illustrate or use some type of graphic organizer before, during, and after their reading to help them find the relationships and key concepts in the text.

Concept mapping, flow charts, idea webs, and other graphic organizers all help students see relationships and get meaning from the text.

This is quite a list for reading engagement. You certainly could have students do all of the above, but most of us can see how different students would find the different strategies of varying personal value. In other words, some students find graphic organizers extremely helpful while others may get more value out of written summaries of text sections.

As a teacher you may want to encourage students to try all of these and perhaps even use all of these on a limited basis, but you also want students to find which of these is most useful to them. In a differentiated classroom, you could offer the students a choice of which of these strategies they want to emphasize. After encouraging or even requiring a taste of all of them, we want students ultimately to focus on which works best for them. This is a terrific thing for students to know about their own learning style, especially college-bound students.

Use Reading Motivation Strategies

Differentiated instruction can assist with the third and equally important reading key, motivation. The research is showing us that increasing motivation for reading involves some simple practices.

1. Establish content goals for reading

Help students decide what types of things they will know after reading that they did not know beforehand.

2. Provide hands-on activities

Reading comprehension is greatly facilitated if students have had some type of hands-on experience with the concept prior to reading. Labs, activities, outings, and other experiential activities prior to reading allow the readers to connect this episodic knowledge with the new information they encounter in the text.

3. Allow student choice in texts

If students are given a choice of topic or subtopic and provided with a choice of books in which to gather their information, both motivation and comprehension increase.

4. Use interesting texts

Books as well as trade publications that have supporting illustrations and logical subsections and chapter divisions can hold students' attention and increase their focus and processing.

5. Use social collaboration

Students learn material better if they are afforded an opportunity to share their learning, questions, and ideas with others. Encourage or assign reading discussion groups.

These motivational strategies, as we saw with the engagement strategies, are easier to operate in a differentiated classroom. Allowing students to have some prereading experiences and some choice in topic and reading material and allowing for small-group interaction are easy to do in any high school classroom. Not only will students be more engaged, but students who are given choices in their learning, and especially choices in their textbooks, do better on assessments (Reynolds & Symons, 2001).

PRACTICE ASSIGNMENTS FOR OVERCOMING THIS OBSTACLE

Practical Solution Idea 17.1: Share with your students the proven ways for engaging themselves with the text.

Require them to try a different one (or two) on each chapter or reading assignment.

Practical Solution Idea 17.2: Use small-group discussions to help them find which way works best for them.

Practical Solution Idea 17.3: Increase motivation by offering a variety of tasks and assignments that pertain to the reading.

Practical Solution Idea 17.4: Introduce reading topics with a hands-on lab.

Practical Solution Idea 17.5: Have students form "book clubs" based on their text choice.

Practical Solution Idea 17.6: Use two or three texts in the room rather than just one.

Practical Solution Idea 17.7: Supplement texts with popular trade publications.

Practical Solution Idea 17.8: Allow plenty of social collaboration on topics pertaining to the reading.

The Bottom Line—If They Are Learning, You Are Teaching

One of the primordial functions of the brain is the acquisition of knowledge.

—Semir Zeki (2004)

From one of my early years as a teacher in Louisiana, I remember the day a colleague came into my room after school in a state of frustration and angst. She was a relatively new teacher, as I was, so we frequently shared our thoughts and ideas. Her statement that day was one I've carried with me for years. "Kathie, I'm so frustrated with these kids. I'm teaching. They're just not learning!"

A DESCRIPTION OF THE ISSUE

Learning means finding a relationship between concepts, developing a skill, or changing a behavior. It requires bringing information into our head, mulling and massaging the information around inside our brain, and then, for school purposes, expressing or demonstrating that learning back out of our heads.

In school we break these processes down into three steps:

- Teaching
- Studying
- Testing

Teaching is the input part. Students listen to lectures, watch videos, read text, or participate in an activity. The point here is to get new information into the brain.

Step two, studying, is the part generally done without the assistance of a teacher. It is an internal process where the students attempt to find cross-references for the new information so that it is assimilated and accommodated into their knowledge bank and mental schemata and can be retrieved or used later.

Testing or assessment is step three. Here the students must demonstrate that the new information has in fact been stored in the brain in such a fashion that it can be recalled or used. It must be demonstrated in a manner sophisticated enough to pass some external measure or criteria.

While complex, this all seems simple enough to most of us because it is a system we are very familiar with. This is our education system, and we are professional educators.

The three-step system seems like a logical model or paradigm. Problems arise, though, with the traditionally narrow range of options and avenues we use for steps one and three. Step one, input, is almost always achieved through linguistic channels. We read the printed word or listen to spoken language: fairly narrow options.

Step three, assessment, is traditionally even more limited and involves several sophisticated skills. Testing is almost always a visual, linguistic, and fine motor activity involving reading printed words and manually writing a representation of our thoughts.

Step one and step three, though, are solely in existence in school for the purpose and benefit of step two, the learning. The bottom line of education is the learning. All the teaching and assessment are all for this bottom line: The Learning. What's really funny is that most of the problems are not due to people struggling with the learning part. Nearly all people can learn things. The brain is set from birth for that: We learn. What causes the problems for most people are parts one and three, the input and the assessment.

Because schools traditionally have been so rigid in the way input and assessment are offered, we actually are limiting the most important step, the learning. It is as though we have lost sight of the real point of education. Schools are here not for the teaching and the assessment; they are here for the learning. So let's focus on that and see if we can't fix some of the problems that come from this conventional rigidness.

SOME STUDENTS STRUGGLE WITH LINGUISTIC-DEPENDENT INPUT AND OUTPUT

My oldest son, Keegan, is an amazing person. He loves to read. Because persons with autism have little value for human emotional relationships, he reads exclusively nonfiction. He reads news magazines and newspapers.

Since the age of 14, he has read the *New York Times* every Sunday. He reads the *Boston Globe* every morning. He reads global political analyses posted on the Internet. His knowledge of what is going on in the world far surpasses mine. He can write a political essay and offer written insights to world politics that would impress just about anyone.

But if you ask him what he did in class this morning in college, he can't tell you. If the phone rings, he won't answer it. He does not do well at processing a college lecture, so he takes courses that can easily be supported with a text. I can ride in a car with him for a three-hour drive, and not a word is exchanged. Keegan has taught me much in the past 21 years about those three steps of school learning.

He can read the most complex information. He can manipulate and process it in his head in order to compare and contrast and analyze. But when it comes time to bring the information back out, don't ask him to send it through the spoken language channels of his brain. That area is a frustration for him. I have witnessed it many times. He will try to express something complex, use the wrong word, stop, and say, "Wait, that's not the right word, oh . . . never mind." Lost are many brilliant thoughts that cannot be turned into spoken words. He can write it, but he can't say it. He can read it but cannot listen to it. Coming in or going out, verbal language is not an avenue for his learning. But he certainly can learn, just not using some of the traditional channels.

SOME STUDENTS STRUGGLE WITH VISUAL INPUT AND OUTPUT

My middle son, Keller, is a brilliant young man too. Since the age of six he has traveled the world with me and sat through many conferences and college lectures on very advanced science and neurological topics. He loves that stuff. His attention never wavers, and he discusses the topics in great detail on the plane ride home. He watches every science documentary he can. He and our town librarian are on a first-name basis as she fulfills his weekly request for an interlibrary loan for audiobooks. He frequently spends much of Saturday listening to his books.

But when Keller has a social studies chapter to read for homework, he brings it to his Dad or me. He can read it himself, but it is an exhausting process and requires so much effort and energy that very little comprehension occurs. His handwriting is illegible, and most of the words are misspelled. Like many people with dyslexia, he finds typing much easier and has learned to use some adaptive technology in school.

So Keller also has problems in school with steps one and three, but they are quite the opposite of the ones his brother has. Keller can listen to the most complex information but struggles to read the simplest material. He has no problem assimilating new information. He certainly can learn.

SOLUTION STRATEGIES

Rethink Our View of Nontraditional Learners

Both of these young men have been labeled learning disabled by the educational system. But the truth is that neither of them is unable to learn. They both can learn a great deal, and both can understand very complex and difficult ideas and concepts.

So perhaps the real story here is that the traditional educational system is what's disabled; disabled in that it frequently has a hard time finding a way to deliver information into some students' brains, and it frequently uses an ineffective way to accurately assess the learning that has occurred.

So students are not learning disabled. Disabled means broken, not working, or "un-able" to learn. I can personally testify that neither of these students falls into that category. We might better call them "nontraditional learners," as opposed to learning disabled.

What is disabled is an education system that cannot effectively teach to a young mind that is perfectly capable of learning.

And so the system is broken for many students. Fortunately there are a great many educators today working hard to fix this system so that it can work for as many students as possible.

PRACTICE ASSIGNMENTS FOR OVERCOMING THIS OBSTACLE

Be Part of the Solution

All of us in education share a special kindred spirit. We all heard the same calling. We chose a profession that does not reward our successes with monetary thanks, holiday bonuses, stock options, or plush offices. We chose a profession that offers other rewards:

The smile of a young person when he or she finally gets it.

The joy that comes from a mission accomplished.

The chance to pass on the passion we feel for learning and for our subject to tomorrow's world.

The opportunity to be a part of so many young lives as they explore and grow.

We change the world, one mind at a time. We are teachers.

The education system has many flaws. It probably always will. But let's never let that dampen our enthusiasm for our profession and the good we can do for our nation's youth. How lucky we are to live in a nation where all people have the opportunity to live their lives with freedom and dignity. Look for creative solutions to the problems we face. Look for ways to help all young people grow and reach their absolute best potential.

Keep forefront in your mind that every child can learn.

Every child.

If we don't believe that, who will?

Suggestions for Further Reading

LAYERED CURRICULUM AND OTHER SPECIFIC STRATEGIES FOR DIFFERENTIATING INSTRUCTION

Erickson, L. (2002). *Concept-based curriculum and instruction: Teaching beyond the facts*. Thousand Oaks, CA: Corwin Press.

Erickson helps teachers design instruction for students to think beyond "facts" and make cross-connections with information for a deeper understanding of the material.

Gregory, G., & Chapman, C. (2002). *Differentiated instructional strategies: One size doesn't fit all*. Thousand Oaks, CA: Corwin Press.

Used frequently as a supplemental education text, this is one of the best overviews of differentiating instruction. The book covers the topic well and includes lots of teacher activity ideas.

Nunley, K. (2004). *Layered Curriculum: The practical solution for teachers with more than one student in their classroom* (2nd ed.). Amherst, NH: BRAINS.org.

Written by this author, who is the developer of the Layered Curriculum method of instruction, this text explains this three-layered method for encouraging higher-level thinking in all students while holding them highly accountable. Examples are given for elementary, middle, and high school classrooms, along with lengthy discussion of the logistic issues involved in running your classroom.

Nunley, K. (2003). *Layered Curriculum: The workbook*. Amherst, NH: BRAINS.org.

This is the workbook companion to the text above. Teachers can complete a unit of Layered Curriculum as well as design grading rubrics and a grading scale.

Sprenger, M. (2003). *Differentiation through learning styles and memory*. Thousand Oaks, CA: Corwin Press.

This book contains ideas for assessing and teaching various learning styles. Assessment inventories are included, along with practical teaching tips for working with your various learners. Easy-to-use information with supporting graphics.

Tomlinson, C. (1999). *The differentiated classroom: Responding to the needs of all learners*. Alexandria, VA: Association for Supervision and Curriculum Development (ASCD).

An easy-to-read, brief overview of how to begin differentiating in your classroom. There are examples and suggestions for a wide range of teaching styles. This book is great for generating teaching ideas.

Tomlinson, C. (2001). *How to differentiate instruction in mixed-ability classrooms* (2nd ed.). Alexandria, VA: ASCD.

This is another excellent book for generating ideas for projects, hands-on activities, and other nontraditional assignments. Tomlinson is one of the leading authors in differentiated instruction.

NEUROSCIENCE AND LEARNING

Howard, P. (1994). *The owner's manual for the brain*. Austin, TX: Leomian Press.

Howard's book jumps quickly back and forth between theory and practice. The book outlines brain theories that have come from research and then gives two or three applications of that research in the real world.

Nunley, K. (2003). *A student's brain: The parent/teacher manual*. Amherst, NH: BRAINS.org.

Written by this author, this book describes, in easy-to-understand language, the workings of the brain. Particular emphasis is put on the adolescent brain, learning disabilities, and suggestions for parents.

Restak, R. (1995). *Brainscapes: An introduction to what neuroscience has learned about the structure, function, and abilities of the brain*. New York: Hyperion Books.

Nice summary of what we "know" about the brain from neuroscience. It is a particularly good read for someone with a basic understanding of the brain who would like a more detailed look at memory, learning, and general neural system functioning.

Sousa, D. (2001). *How the brain learns*. Thousand Oaks, CA: Corwin Press.

Sousa was one of the pioneers in writing on neuroscience for educators. This books gives a good basic outline of how the brain functions and of key issues in neuropsychology as they relate to education.

Sylwester, R. (1995). *A celebration of neurons: An educator's guide to the human brain.* Alexandria, VA: ASCD.

> One of the books that started the "brain-based learning" interest in education. The book is a great starting point for your journey.

Sylwester, R. (2003). *A biological brain in a cultural classroom* (2nd ed.). Thousand Oaks, CA: Corwin Press.

> This book is excellent for reexamining the role and relationship between students and teachers in the classroom. Sylwester uses his deep understanding of brain function to explain learning, discovery, and classroom management.

Wolfe, P. (2001). *Brain matters: Translating research into classroom practice.* Alexandria, VA: ASCD.

> This book starts with an excellent overview of the workings of the brain, including neuron function and the role of neurotransmitters. Wolfe concludes with some practical application of this theory in the classroom.

INCLUSION STRATEGIES

Lewis, R., & Doorlag, D. (1995). *Teaching special students in the mainstream.* Englewood Cliffs, NJ: Prentice Hall.

> This generous guide gives the reader an overview of various exceptionalities and modification ideas that can be carried out by the regular classroom teacher. While the book focuses more on individual modifications than on whole-class modifications, it has a wealth of ideas and is a great reference.

Rief, S., & Heimburge, J. (1996). *How to reach and teach all students in the inclusive classroom.* West Nyack, NY: The Center for Applied Research in Education.

> This books give a nice overview of learning styles, multiple intelligences, and various exceptionalities in the classroom, including giftedness. The book is loaded with examples, teaching ideas, lesson plans, and suggestions for a wide range of teaching subjects.

Stowe, C. (2000). *How to reach and teach children and teens with dyslexia.* San Francisco: Jossey-Bass.

> The book is a great resource for anyone working with struggling readers from the middle grades on up. There are practical activities and strategies for helping improve reading and writing skills as well as compensation strategies.

CONTROL THEORY AND SELF-EFFICACY

Bandura, A. (1997). *Self-efficacy: The exercise of control.* New York: W. H. Freeman.

> While this book may be difficult to obtain, it is the basic book on Bandura's work on self-efficacy. He has others which deal with the same

topic. Bandura writes on the event of self-efficacy and how you can develop it in others. For teachers who want their students to believe in themselves and in their own abilities.

Csikszentmihalyi, M. (1997). *Creativity: Flow and the psychology of discovery and invention*. New York: HarperCollins.

How are creative people creative? What makes a creative person? Csikszentmihalyi uses interviews with dozens of creative people to support his theories on creativity, happiness, and flow.

Csikszentmihalyi, M. (1997). *Finding flow*. New York: Basic Books.

This book, as the one above, is by one of the leading writers on learned optimism, positive psychology, and happiness. The author covers the idea of happiness and intrinsic reward systems in what he terms "flow." Csikszentmihalyi is known for his work and theories on happiness and why it does not correlate with wealth and material goods.

Dewey, J. (1937). *Experience in education*. New York: Macmillan.

Dewey's work continues to be reprinted today, which makes a statement in itself. The so-called father of constructivism, Dewey explains why education needs to be authentic and experiential.

Glasser, W. (1990). *The quality school: Managing students without coercion*. New York: Perennial Library.
Glasser, W., & Dotson, K. (1998). *Choice theory in the classroom*. New York: Harper.

Both of these books by Glasser are my recommendations for teachers looking for alternative strategies in classroom management. As we know, punishment-based systems are ineffective, but what are our options? Glasser gives you practical strategies for nonaversive classroom management.

Hunter, M. (1990). *Discipline that develops self-discipline*. Thousand Oaks, CA: Corwin Press.

The book for teachers who are tired of punishment-based systems. Hunter shows you how to help your students control their own behavior and be responsible.

Lambert, N., & McCombs, B. (Eds.). (1998). *How students learn: Reforming schools through learner-centered education*. Washington, DC: American Psychological Association.

This volume includes current research by educational psychologists in the field of student learning and presents their perspective on what changes need to occur in classrooms. One of the best books on education from a psychological-learning perspective.

Levine, M. (2002). *A mind at a time*. New York: Simon & Schuster.

Levine writes for parents and teachers and gives insights into appreciating the strengths of all children as well as various ways to view giftedness and traditional views of learning disabilities.

McCombs, B., & Whisler, J. (1997). *The learner-centered classroom and school: Strategies for increasing student motivation and achievement*. San Francisco: Jossey-Bass.

This book covers not only the how and why of student-centered classrooms but practical strategies for classroom management as well.

PEDAGOGICAL THEORY

Armstrong, T. (1998). *Awakening genius in the classroom*. Alexandria, VA: ASCD.

Armstrong's writing here encourages educators to really step back, slow down, and view their mission in a different light. The book is an easy read with practical suggestions and ideas for helping students find their inner genius and creativity.

Brooks, J., & Brooks, M. (1999). *In search of understanding: The case for constructivist classrooms* (2nd ed.). Alexandria, VA: ASCD.

The authors help teachers set up classrooms where students discover and come to a deeper understanding of the learning objectives. The book contains practical ideas for engaging even reluctant learners.

Gardner, H. (1993). *Multiple intelligences: The theory in practice*. New York: Basic Books.

This is a collection of academic essays intended as a follow-up to Gardner's *Intelligence Reframed*. The book reviews recent advances in cognitive studies and neuroscience, along with their applications in the classroom.

Gardner, H. (1999). *Intelligence reframed: Multiple intelligences for the 21st century*. New York: Basic Books.

How would Mozart have done on the SAT or GRE? Gardner puts multiple intelligences into historical perspective, reviewing the history of modern intelligence. Includes Gardner's prescribed curriculum.

Healy, J. (1992). *Endangered minds: Why our children don't think*. New York: Simon & Schuster.

A classic, in-depth discussion of brain development in children and how modern society may be harmful to the process. Healy takes a different but interesting view of how even educational television can be bad for the developing mind by means of its delivery of a constant bombardment of rather empty external stimuli.

Marzano, R. (2003). *What works in schools: Translating research into action.* Alexandria, VA: ASCD.

Works to show how research of the past few decades can be used in the classroom for a dramatic improvement in public education. Marzano takes a wide-ranging view, exploring factors from community and parents to teachers and students.

Sternberg, R. (1985). *Beyond IQ: A triarchic theory of human intelligence.* New York: Cambridge University Press.

Sternberg is one of the foremost experts on traditional views of intelligence. This book examines his three-component system and includes a discussion of the best measure of intelligence.

Wiggins, G., & McTighe, J. (1998). *Understanding by design.* Alexandria, VA: ASCD.

These authors pose that teachers need to help their students understand that knowledge and learning is not always neat and clean and sequential. Rather, real-world "knowledge" is frequently beset by controversies and inconsistencies.

HISTORY OF THE UNITED STATES SCHOOL SYSTEM

Angus, D., & Mirel, J. (1999).*The failed promise of the American high school, 1890–1995.* New York: Teachers College Press.

The books gives a unique perspective on the history of the American high school. The book is an excellent source for data and trends in high school in the last century.

Feldman, R. (2001). *Don't whistle in school: The history of America's public schools.* Minneapolis, MN: Lerner Publications.

Covers the history of schools in the United States from the dawn of our school system through modern controversies.

Nasaw, D. (1979). *Schooled to order: A social history of public schooling in the United States.* Oxford, UK: Oxford University Press.

An excellent summary of the political history of America's school system including our higher education system.

Weis, L. (1988). *Class, race and gender in American education.* Albany: State University of New York Press.

This is a volume of essays on socioeconomic class, ethnic group issues, gender, and other concerns in the history of American schools.

CLASSROOM AND SCHOOL LEADERSHIP

Glickman, C. (2002). *Leadership for learning: How to help teachers succeed.* Alexandria, VA: ASCD.

> Updated and straightforward strategies for principals, teachers, and other leaders in education to use for creating change in the classroom. The emphasis is on improving teaching and learning through different structures, formats, and approaches.

Senge, P., Kleiner, A., Roberts, C., Ross, R., & Smith, B. (1994). *The fifth discipline fieldbook: Strategies and tools for building a learning organization.* New York: Doubleday.

> A large collection of articles by consultants specializing in creating change within organizations. A classic in the corporate world, this work is very accessible and includes a very large selection of ideas and approaches.

Wheatley, M. (1994). *Leadership and the new science.* San Francisco: Berrett-Koehler.

> This updated edition of Wheatley's cutting-edge work of the early 1990s offers a clearer explanation of her ideas on how chaos theory and quantum physics can be applied to understanding the dynamics of an organization. While this sounds highly theoretical, Wheatley brings it down to earth with many practical examples relating to a variety of organizational types.

References

Adelson, R. (2004). Hormones, stress and aggression—A vicious cycle. *Monitor on Psychology* (APA), *35*(10), 18–19.

Armstrong, T. (1999). *7 kinds of smart: Identifying and developing your multiple intelligences.* New York: Penguin Putnam.

Asch, S. (1955). *Opinions and social pressure.* Scientific American, vol. 193(5), pg. 31–35.

Asche, S. (1956). *Studies of independence and conformity: A minority of one against a unanimous majority.* Psychological Monographs, 70, number 9.

Atwater, M. (1995). The multicultural science classroom. *The Science Teacher*, *62*(4), 42–45.

Bennis, W., & Nanus, B. (1997). *Leaders: Strategies for taking charge.* New York: HarperCollins.

Benware, C., & Deci, E. (1984). The quality of learning with an active versus passive motivational set. *American Educational Research Journal*, *21*, 755–765.

Berson, Y., & Linton, J. (2005). An examination of the relationships between leadership style, quality, and employee satisfaction in R&D versus administrative environments. *R & D Management*, *35*(1), 51–61.

Blumenfeld, P., et al. (1991). Motivating project-based learning: Sustaining the doing, supporting the learning. *Educational Psychologist*, *26*, 369–398.

Boggiano, A. K., et al. (1993). Use of techniques promoting students' self-determination: Effects on students' analytic problem-solving skills. *Motivation and Emotion*, *17*, 319–336.

Bond, R., & Smith, P. (1996). Culture and conformity: A meta-analysis of studies using Asch's (1952b, 1956) line judgment task. *Psychological Bulletin*, *119*(1), 111–137.

Braten, I., & Samuelstuen, M. (2004). Does the influence of reading purpose on reports of strategic text processing depend on students' topic knowledge? *Journal of Educational Psychology*, *96*(2), 324–336.

Canfield, J., & Siccone, F. (1993). *101 Ways to develop student self-esteem and responsibility.* Needham Heights, MA: Allyn & Bacon.

Christakis, D., et al. (2004). Early television exposure and subsequent attention problems in children. *Pediatrics*, *113*(4), 708–713.

Cutts, N., & Moseley, N. (1960). *Providing for individual difference in the elementary school.* Englewood Cliffs, NJ: Prentice Hall.

Deci, E. (1995). *Why we do what we do: The dynamics of personal autonomy.* New York: Grosset/Putnam.

Deci, E., & Ryan, R. (1985). *Intrinsic motivation and self determination in human behavior*. New York: Plenum Press.

Dickson, M., et al. (2003). Research on leadership in a cross-cultural context: Making progress, and raising new questions. *Leadership Quarterly, 14*(6), 729–769.

Do, S., & Schallert, D. (2004). Emotions and classroom talk: Toward a model of the role of affect in students' experiences of classroom discussions. *Journal of Educational Psychology, 96*(4), 619–634.

Dolezal, S., et al. (2003). How nine third-grade teachers motivate student academic engagement. *Elementary School Journal, 103*, 239–267.

Doyle, W. (1983). Academic work. *Review of Educational Research, 53*, 159–199.

Duman, R., et al. (1999). Neural plasticity to stress and antidepressant treatment. *Biological Psychiatry, 46*(9), 1181–1191.

Dyck, J. (1994, November). The case for the L-shaped classroom: Does the shape of a classroom affect the quality of the learning that goes inside it? *Principal*, 41–45.

Emans, B., et al. (2003). Constructive consequences of leaders forcing influence styles. *Applied Psychology: An International Review, 52*(1), 36–44.

Fang, Z. (1996). A review of research on teacher beliefs and practices. *Educational Research, 38*, 47–65.

Feiman-Nemser, S., et al. (1989). *Changing beginning teachers' conceptions: A description of an introductory teacher education course* (Research Report No. 89-1). East Lansing, MI: National Center for Research on Teacher Education.

Flink, C., et al. (1992). Children's achievement-related behaviors: The role of extrinsic and intrinsic motivational orientations. In A. K. Boggiano & T. S. Pittman (Eds.), *Achievement and motivation: A social-developmental perspective* (pp. 189–214). New York: Cambridge University Press.

Fry, E. (1983). *The reading teacher's book of lists*. Englewood Cliffs, NJ: Prentice Hall.

Good, H., & Teller, J. (1973). *A history of American education*. New York: Macmillan.

Goslin, D. (2003). *Engaging minds: Motivation and learning in America's schools*. Oxford, UK: Scarecrow Education.

Grossman, P. (1990). *The making of a teacher: Teacher knowledge and teacher education*. New York: Teachers College Press.

Guthrie, J., et al. (2004). Increasing reading comprehension and engagement through concept oriented reading instruction. *Journal of Educational Psychology, 96*(3), 403–423.

Hargreaves, J., & Gray, S. (1983). Changing teachers' practice: Innovation and ideology in a part-time B.Ed. course. *Journal of Education for Teaching, 9*, 161–183.

Harris, J. (1995). Sheltered instruction. *The Science Teacher, 62*(2), 24–27.

Howard, P. (1994). *The owner's manual for the brain*. Austin, TX: Leomian Press.

Johnson, W., & Ridley, C. (2004). *The elements of mentoring*. New York: Palgrave Macmillan.

Jones, G., & Vesilind, E. (1996). Putting practice into theory: Changes in the organization of preservice teachers' pedagogical knowledge. *American Educational Research Journal, 33*, 91–117.

Keegan, M. (1995). Psychological and physiological mechanisms by which discovery and didactic methods work. *School Science and Mathematics, 95*(1), 3–10.

Kern, L., et al. (2001). Choice of task sequence to reduce behavior problems. *Journal of Positive Behavior Interventions, 3*(1), 3–10.

King, P., & Kitchener, K. (1994). *Developing reflective judgment: Understanding and promoting intellectual growth and critical thinking in adolescents and adults*. San Francisco: Jossey-Bass.

Koene, B., et al. (2002). Leadership effects on organizational climate and financial performance: Local leadership effect in chain organizations. *Leadership Quarterly, 13*(3), 193–218.

Kotter, J. (1988). *The leadership factor*. New York: The Free Press.

Kouzes, J., & Posner, B. (1996). *The leadership challenge: How to keep getting extraordinary things done in organizations*. San Francisco: Jossey-Bass.

Lambert, N., & McCombs, B. (1998). *How students learn: Reforming schools through learner-centered instruction*. Washington, DC: American Psychological Association.

Levine, M. (2002). *A mind at a time: America's top learning expert shows how every child can succeed*. New York: Simon & Schuster.

Lewin, K., & Lippitt, R. (1938). An experimental approach to the study of autocracy and democracy: A preliminary note. *Sociometry, 11*, 292–300.

Lewin, K., Lippitt, R., & White, R. (1939). Patterns of aggressive behaviour in experimentally created social climates. *Journal of Social Psychology, 10*, 271–299.

Lodewyk, K., & Winne, P. (2005). Relations among the structure of learning tasks, achievement, and changes in self-efficacy in secondary students. *Journal of Educational Psychology, 197*(1), 3–12.

Lok, P., & Crawford, J. (2004). The effect of organisational culture and leadership style on job satisfaction and organisational commitment: A cross-national comparison. *Journal of Management Development, 23*(4), 321–339.

Manning, M. L., & Lucking, R. (1990). Ability grouping: Realities and alternatives. *Childhood Education, 66*(4), 254–258.

McClintick, D. (2000, October 30). The great American textbook scandal. *Forbes*, 178–183.

McCruddeen, M., et al. (2005). The effect of relevance instructions on reading time and learning. *Journal of Educational Psychology, 97*(1), 88–102.

McEwen, B., & Magarinos, A. (2001). Stress and hippocampal plasticity: Implications for the pathophysiology of affective disorders. *Human Psychopharmacology, 16*(1), S7-S19.

Meek, A. (Ed.). (1995). *Designing places for learning*. Alexandria, VA: ASCD.

Morrison, H. (1926). *The practice of teaching in the secondary school*. Chicago: University of Chicago Press.

National Association of Secondary School Principals. (2005). NASSP's view on high school reform. *Secondary School Improvement*. Retrieved May 17, 2005, from www.principals.org/

National Commission on Excellence in Education. (1983). *A nation at risk*. Washington, DC: U.S. Department of Education.

National Reading Panel. (2000). *Teaching children to read: An evidence based assessment of the scientific research literature on reading and its implications for reading instruction*. Washington, DC: National Institute of Child Health and Human Development.

Nunley, K. (1996). *Increasing time on task and decreasing failure rates in high school biology by variations in teaching strategies* (A Practicum I Report presented to Nova Southeastern University, Fort Lauderdale, FL).

Nunley, K. (2002). Active research leads to active classrooms. *Principal Leadership* (National Association of Secondary School Principals), 2(7), 53–56.

Nunley, K. (2003a). *A student's brain: The parent/teacher manual*. Amherst, NH: BRAINS.org.

Nunley, K. (2003b). Giving credit where credit is due. *Principal Leadership* (National Association of Secondary School Principals), *3*(9), 26–31.

Nunley, K. (2004). *Layered Curriculum: The practical solution for teachers with more than one student in their classroom* (2nd ed.). Amherst, NH: BRAINS.org.

O'Reilly, R., & Rudy, J. (2000). Computational principles of learning in the neocortex and hippocampus. *Hippocampus, 10,* 389–397.

Olff, M. (1999). Stress, depression and immunity: The role of defense and coping styles. *Psychiatry Research, 85*(1), 7–15.

Ozgungor, S., & Guthrie, J. (2004). Interactions among elaborative interrogation, knowledge, and interest in the process of constructing knowledge from text. *Journal of Educational Psychology, 96,* 437–443.

Patrick, B., Skinner, E., & Connell, J. (1993). What motivates children's behavior and emotion? Joint effects of perceived control and autonomy in the academic domain. *Journal of Personality and Social Psychology, 65,* 781–791.

Pauley, E. (1991). *The classroom crucible: What really works, what doesn't and why.* New York: Basic Books.

Perry, N. (1998). Young children's self-regulated learning and contexts that support it. *Journal of Educational Psychology, 90,* 715–729.

Pine, D., et al. (1999). Memory and anxiety in prepubertal boys at risk for delinquency. *Journal of American Academy of Child and Adolescent Psychiatry, 38*(8), 1024–1031.

Pressley, M. (2000). What should comprehension instruction be the instruction of? In M. L. Kamil, P. B. Mosenthal, P. D. Pearson, & R. Barr (Eds.), *Handbook of reading research,* vol. 3 (pp. 545–561). Mahwah, NJ: Erlbaum.

Raudenbush, S., et al. (1993). Higher order instructional goals in secondary schools: Class, teacher and school influences. *American Educational Research Journal, 30,* 523–553.

Reeve, J., Bolt, E., & Cai, Y. (1999). Autonomy-supportive teachers: How they teach and motivate students. *Journal of Educational Psychology, 91*(3), 537–548.

Renyi, J. (1993). The arts and humanities in American education. In R. Jennings (Ed.), *Fire in the eyes of youth: The humanities in American education* (pp. 1–13). St. Paul, MN: Occasional Press.

Renzulli, J., Reis, S., & Smith, L. (1981). *The revolving door identification model.* Mansfield Center, CT: Creative Learning Press.

Restak, R. (1995). *Brainscapes: An introduction to what neuroscience has learned about the structure, function, and abilities of the brain.* New York: Hyperion Books.

Reudenbush, S., et al. (1993). Higher order instructional goals in secondary schools: Class, teacher and school influences. *American Educational Research Journal, 30,* 523–553.

Reynolds, P., & Symons, S. (2001). Motivational variables and children's text search. *Journal of Educational Psychology, 93,* 14–23.

Rosenthal, R. (1991). Teacher expectancy effects: A brief update 25 years after the Pygmalion experiment. *Journal of Research in Education, 1,* 3–12.

Rosenthal, R., & Jacobson, L. (1992). *Pygmalion in the classroom: Teacher expectation and pupils' intellectual development.* New York: Irvington.

Ryan, A., et al., (1998). Why do some students avoid asking for help? An examination of the interplay among students' academic efficacy, teachers' social-emotional role and the classroom goal structure. *Journal of Educational Psychology, 90*(3), 528–535.

Shaywitz, S. (2003). *Overcoming dyslexia: A new and complete science-based program for reading problems at any level*. New York: Knopf.

Skopec, E., & Smith, D. (1997). *The practical executive and team building*. Chicago: NTC Publishing.

Sousa, D. (2001). *How the brain learns*. Thousand Oaks, CA: Corwin Press.

Sparks, G. (1988). Teachers' attitudes toward change and subsequent improvements in classroom teaching. *Journal of Educational Psychology, 80,* 111–117.

Stainback, S., & Stainback, W. (1992). *Curriculum considerations in inclusive classrooms: Facilitating learning for all students*. Baltimore, MD: Paul H. Brookes.

Stipek, D. (2002). Good instruction is motivating. In A. Wigfield & J. S. Eccles (Eds.), *Development of achievement motivation* (pp. 309–332). San Diego, CA: Academic Press.

Sylwester, R. (1995). *A celebration of neurons: An educator's guide to the human brain*. Alexandria, VA: ASCD.

Sylwester, R. (2003). *A biological brain in a cultural classroom* (2nd ed.). Thousand Oaks, CA: Corwin Press.

Tervaniemi, M., & Hugdahl, K. (2003). Lateralization of auditory-cortex function. *Brain Research Reviews, 43*(3), 231–246.

Tomlinson, C. (1995). *How to differentiate instruction in mixed-ability classrooms*. Alexandria, VA: ASCD.

Tomlinson, C. (2001). *How to differentiate instruction in mixed-ability classrooms* (2nd ed.). Alexandria, VA: ASCD.

Torff, B. (2003). Developmental changes in teachers' use of higher order thinking and content knowledge. *Journal of Educational Psychology, 95,* 563–569.

Torff, B. (2005). Developmental changes in teachers' beliefs about critical-thinking activities. *Journal of Educational Psychology, 97*(1), 13–22.

U.S. Bureau of the Census. (2000). Graduation rates by race 1940–today. Retrieved April 2004, from http://www.census.gov/population/socdemo/education/tabA-2.pdf

Vallerand, R., Fortier, M., & Guay, F. (1997). Self-determination and persistence in a real-life setting: Toward a motivational model of high school dropout. *Journal of Personality and Social Psychology, 72,* 1161–1176.

van Engen, M., et al. (2001). Gender, context and leadership styles: A field study. *Journal of Occupational & Organizational Psychology, 74*(5), 581–599.

Vansteenkiste, M., et al. (2004). Less is sometimes more: Content matters. *Journal of Educational Psychology, 96*(4), 735–764.

Veenstra, K., et al. (2003). A social identity and leadership: A new look at the role of leadership style. *Australian Journal of Psychology, 55,* 66–72.

von Oech, R. (1990). *A whack on the side of the head*. New York: Warner Books.

Walls, T., & Little, T. (2005). Relations among personal agency, motivation and school adjustment in early adolescence. *Journal of Educational Psychology, 97*(1), 23–31.

Weaver, R. (1990). Separate is not equal. *Principal, 69*(5), 40–42.

Wigfield, A., & Tonks, S. (2004). The development of motivation for reading and how it is influenced by CORI. In J. T. Guthrie, A. Wigfield, & K. C. Perencevich (Eds.), *Motivating reading comprehension: Concept-oriented reading instruction* (pp. 249–272). Mahwah, NJ: Erlbaum.

Wilcox, B. (1982). *Design of high school programs for severely handicapped students*. Baltimore, MD: Paul Brooks.

Willis, S. (1995, summer). *Reinventing science education: Reformers promote hands-on, inquiry-based learning. Curriculum Update.* Alexandria, VA: ASCD.

Winebrenner, S. (2000). Gifted students need an education, too. *Educational Leadership* (ASCD), *58*(1), 52–56.

Wyers, W., Dohm, B., & Ayers, R. (Eds.). (2001). *Zero tolerance: Resisting the drive for punishment in our schools.* New York: The New Press.

Zeki, S. (2004). The neurology of ambiguity. *Consciousness & Cognition, 13*(1), 173–196.

Zohar, A., & Dori, J. (2003). Higher order thinking and low-achieving students: Are they mutually exclusive? *Journal of the Learning Sciences, 12,* 145–182.

Zohar, A., et al. (2001). Teachers' beliefs about low-achieving students and higher-order thinking. *Teaching and Teacher Education, 17,* 469–485.

Index

**CORWIN
PRESS**

The Corwin Press logo—a raven striding across an open book—represents the union of courage and learning. Corwin Press is committed to improving education for all learners by publishing books and other professional development resources for those serving the field of PreK–12 education. By providing practical, hands-on materials, Corwin Press continues to carry out the promise of its motto: **"Helping Educators Do Their Work Better."**